David Voss

THE CHALLENGE

Reinhold Messner

THE CHALLENGE

Translated by Noel Bowman
and Audrey Salkeld

KAYE & WARD · LONDON
OXFORD UNIVERSITY PRESS · NEW YORK

PHOTOGRAPHS

Black & White

Aldo Anghileri, p 22; E-Buhl, p 151; Riccardo Cassin, p 9; Peter Habeler, p 171, 188, 192; Lamberto Londi, p 98; Fosco Maraini, p 163; Reinhold Messner, p 19, 33, 42, 64, 67, 71, 90, 95, 107, 167, 186; Vittorio Sella, p 137, 138/139, 140/141, 143, 146, 148/149.

Coloured Photographs

All taken by Reinhold Messner with the exception of the last three (by Peter Habeler)

First published in Great Britain by
Kaye & Ward Ltd.
21 New Street, London EC2M 4NT
1977

First published in the USA by
Oxford University Press Inc.
200 Madison Avenue, New York, N.Y. 10016
1977

ISBN 0 7182 1159 6 (Great Britain)
ISBN 0-19-519974-X   (USA)
Library of Congress Catalog Card No. 77-77793

Printed in Great Britain by
Whitstable Litho Ltd, Whitstable, Kent

CONTENTS

LHOTSE

INTERLUDE

HIDDEN PEAK

PUBLISHER'S NOTE

The height of peaks and length of routes, etc., are given in metres, partly because this is how they appear in the author's German original, and also because it is becoming increasingly common in the English-speaking world to use metric terms. Readers may, however, find it helpful to consult the approximate conversion table given below.

$$
\begin{aligned}
1 \text{ metre} &= 3.28 \text{ feet} \\
100 \text{ metres} &= 328.00 \text{ feet} \\
1000 \text{ metres} &= 3281.00 \text{ feet} \\
2000 \text{ metres} &= 6562.00 \text{ feet} \\
3000 \text{ metres} &= 9843.00 \text{ feet} \\
4000 \text{ metres} &= 13124.00 \text{ feet} \\
5000 \text{ metres} &= 16404.00 \text{ feet} \\
6000 \text{ metres} &= 19685.00 \text{ feet} \\
7000 \text{ metres} &= 22966.00 \text{ feet} \\
8000 \text{ metres} &= 26247.00 \text{ feet}
\end{aligned}
$$

LHOTSE

CONFLICT

Morning shimmered through the roof of the tent as the sun's first rays caught its slack, faded canvas. I shivered. These cold sluggish hours before sun-up were always damned unpleasant. I was only half awake and fragments of dreams kept floating to the surface of my consciousness. But though the details escaped me I was aware of an overwhelming sadness, as if I had lost the woman I loved. Suddenly as a last wave of sleep swept over me, a complete picture etched itself in my mind: A hotel lobby, a Persian carpet, a Kirchner print on the wall. A woman was searching for someone – not desperately nor in an agitated manner, but with the quiet persistence of an animal looking for its young. She wore a long dress with no belt, she was slender with a fabulous figure. Obviously it had been her children for whom she sought as she came back some moments later with two small boys and clasping a little girl by the hand. They went outside and disappeared down the street. Only for a moment did her glance meet mine – I saw turquoise eyes in a face, which, though it lacked the perfect lines of a photographer's model, was hauntingly beautiful all the same. There was a hint of melancholy about her, a sensual warmth. The woman in the picture had neither her face nor her figure, and moreover wore her hair quite differently, yet I fancied I could see a resemblance between the two. Perhaps they shared the same destiny?

A shaft of light found its way through the half-open door of the tent and I rolled over in my sleeping bag to avoid its glare. Drowsily for a few moments more, I clung to the strange image of my dream. Then without opening my eyes, I fumbled for the altimeter which the night before I had hung up above my head. My fingers closed round it and I struggled to open my eyes which were smarting badly. I squinted at the dial: "5,300 metres", I said it half aloud, forgetting for a moment that I was not alone in the tent and that my companion, Aldo Anghileri, was still asleep. But he didn't wake up; he just grunted and went on sleeping, smiling peacefully. In my head I tried to work out by how much the barometer must have fallen for the altimeter to be registering

Everest (8848m) and Lhotse (8511m) from the south. Both summits are separated from one another by the South Col, (7986m).

60 metres higher than the previous evening; I turned the expensive instrument over in its dark brown leather case and read the inscription on the back: "To the Conqueror of Eight-thousanders from his Friends in the CAI Belledo Section, 29.10.74".

"Conqueror of Eight-thousanders", I thought "And so sleepy!" Last autumn I had given a lecture to the members of the CAI Belledo, the Lecco Section of the Italian Alpine Club, and it was there that I had met both my tent companion, Aldo Anghileri, and the leader of our Lhotse Expedition, Riccardo Cassin. The altimeter was presented to me at the meeting by Renato Frigerio, an old friend of mine and a leading light in this very active club. He concluded his speech with the words "Take it with you on all future expeditions."

He was thinking in particular of the Italian Lhotse South Face Expedition, which a few weeks before I had been invited to join, and hoping that the summit of Lhotse would become my third success on an eight-thousand metre peak, following Nanga Parbat and Manaslu.

Now, six months later, we had reached a height of 6,400 metres but the hope that we would have success on the Lhotse Face was fading. Remembering how our Makalu South Face expedition had foundered the previous year, it seemed that our chances on this much more serious Lhotse South Face, must be reckoned as nil; the inscription on the altimeter seemed now to be ironically optimistic.

Meanwhile Aldo had also woken up, but it was only after I had wished him good morning and told him that we could expect bad weather, that he realised that he was here in Base Camp under the Lhotse Face and not back home in Italy with his wife. "Good God!" he paused, then "We must be mad." After which outburst, he laughed aloud. But as quickly became solemn again. The smile froze on his lips and he plucked at his half-grown beard, which was obviously irritating him.

"What on earth am I doing here?" he queried, as if the seriousness of the expedition had only just then dawned upon him. He thought over the last strenuous weeks, how his legs hadn't been able to work as fast as they used to, how he hadn't been able to keep up with Mario Curnis when the two of them were fixing ropes on the difficult stretches between Camps I and II. Aldo felt that he personally had no chance of making it to the summit. He could only hope to be a back-up member of the team, to fix ropes and so forth, and this he wasn't content to be.

He thought of his tender blonde wife, how she hadn't wanted him to come on this expedition and had implored him to stay at home; then he thought of his children and mechanically picked up his diary in which he kept some photographs of them. He passed them across to me, one by one, telling me the children's names and something about each of them. If a few minutes before I was in some doubt what was going on in Aldo's mind, I knew now. "I must tell you something", he began again after a short pause, and his face which had become so alive as he talked about his children, clouded over again. "I can't – I can't stand it any more." The words broke out of him with the full force of the hopelessness he felt.

He stared at me with desperate eyes, hoping perhaps that I would laugh him out of it. I now remembered that several times in the last few days he had said he would quit and go back to Europe, but we had all thought he was only joking.

"We are all mad to risk our necks for such a rock-face as this." Now I could see this was no joke. What he had been doing before was testing what our reactions would be, and in particular the reaction of our leader, Cassin, should he jack it all in.

"Can I just go?"

"But why pull out now?"

"Because I've had a bellyful that's why."

I sensed he felt guilty at having accepted a place on the team in the first place. It was tormenting him.

"You can go home any time you like." I said. "So what that you agreed to come? You can just as easily change your mind." I was trying to clarify the position in his mind.

Aldo is a very competent mountaineer indeed. It is true that he hadn't been on a large expedition before and perhaps he was over-hasty in accepting a place on this one, but he was fully qualified for such an undertaking as the Lhotse South Face.

He had made a number of first ascents throughout the length and breadth of the Alps, as well as some early repeats of great classical routes, also winter ascents, mostly in the Western Alps, and the swift-est ever solo ascent of the Badile North-east Face in the Val Bregaglia. It took just two and a half hours to polish off this 900 metre granite wall, and the whole alpine world had sat up and taken notice.

Aldo is small of build, stocky, with a narrow face. He has done all sorts of jobs in his time. Once he had his own big engineering busi-ness, but it went bankrupt. Now he is a sales representative. But most of all he is a mountaineer and a spectacular rock-climber. His climbing successes he owed rather more to his boldness and his ability to move fast, than to stamina or subtlety.

Since neither of us could face getting up and washing in the icy stream outside, we stayed in bed a bit longer. All round us was a chaos of gear – down trousers, helmets, boots, shirts. On the tent poles more bits and pieces were hung and in cardboard boxes at the foot of our sleeping mats, we had stuffed all the things we didn't expect to need either on the face or in Base Camp.

"I wonder what my wife's doing right now?"

"Sleeping", I said.

"Yes I guess so – it's only 3 o'clock in Italy."

Then Aldo suddenly began to read me passages from his diary which was still lying beside him. Some of his photos fell out and slipped between our two air mattresses. I fished them out while he read:

"I don't know why I ever wanted to climb this mountain at all. Life here, at the moment, makes me quite sick. If I think about it, I can see that it's weakness on my part, that I have allowed a longing for my wife and children to over-power any climbing ambitions I once had. It is not so bad when I'm kept busy, but when I'm inactive, when the teams change over and bad weather pins us down in Base Camp, then all sorts of thoughts go round and round in my head.

11

I am sure – I feel it – that a different set of motivations influence us on an expedition than on an alpine climb. Here everything is regulated, worked out in advance – so much effort, so much food, so much sleep. It's all compulsory. We do it, but we don't experience it, it just happens to us. Chance doesn't come into it, it's all pre-ordained."

I didn't agree with this entirely and would have said something, but Aldo went on reading.

"Certainly this expedition is a great adventure, but I can't help wondering whether it wouldn't be better to spend four or five days climbing an alpine face and putting everything one has got into it. All one's skill and enthusiasm for a single experience. Aesthetics don't count for much out here. There is no style: nobody can climb elegantly at high altitude. I cannot see what such an expedition can offer, even to Cassin. What good are his free-climbing skills here? He might just as well have been a lesser alpinist. The only things that count here are willpower – and that to the extent of brutality to oneself – organisation and cold reckoning. I say all this not in any way as an excuse or a let-out for me, but because these are my personal observations."

These few passages that Aldo had scribbled in his diary on 28th March, 1975, convinced me he was really serious about going home. I could sympathise with his point of view, probably because I had often been in similar situations myself. On my various expeditions I have been with over a hundred men, and have lived through many doubts and crises. I know what it means to be separated from one's wife for two or three months at a time, and not to have one's best and most trusted friends around. One never gets used to it. It is just as hard an adjustment each and every time. This Lhotse expedition was all in all my fourteenth, so I could not be said to lack experience; even so when thinking about it before I came away, I had expected it to be easier, much easier. Quite apart from the loneliness and the desire for tenderness which is never fulfilled, expedition life is a continual struggle against dirt, cold and fatigue. I could understand Aldo's dilemma all too well, understand how desperate he felt, torn between homesickness and ambition.

"You're right." I said, "Completely right. You're not the first person to feel like this on an expedition, but you may be the first to have had the courage to say what you felt out loud, and to face up to the possible consequences of abandoning an expedition."

"If you climb mountains because you enjoy it, because you get some relaxation from it, then this is the wrong place and the wrong mountain!" Aldo was vehement.

*Authentic extracts from the private diary of Aldo Anghileri.

"The relaxation and the pleasure comes later surely, after the effort", I said.

"After three months? Only to the people who actually make the summit, I suspect. Bloody hell!"

After a bit, he read some more:

"One might expect the pleasure from such an expedition to be in direct proportion to the size of the undertaking, but I am not convinced that this is so. I have some very good memories of my winter epic on the Gugliermina this year and of many other tours, but I cannot believe there is a single mountain that could so occupy a man's life, that it can fulfil him and hold him in thrall for months on end. Such a venture would only be logical if you knew that the heights to which you aspired, could be attained and without undue danger or difficulty. If, however, you let yourself get carried away by your great endeavour and attack your mountain with superhuman efforts, then it becomes nothing more nor less than a big ego-trip."

"Perhaps you don't understand the challenge", I broke in, "the challenge that a great face like this can have for a climber."

But Aldo answered with typical Italian passion:

"Can any face be worth giving up so much for? I don't mean giving up material things, I'm thinking of the sacrifice of not seeing your children for three or four months. My children are now 2 and 4 years old, and I can never again see them as they are now. I love playing with them – what I wouldn't give to be with them now! And my wife, who I know must be feeling our separation every bit as keenly as I am."

Meanwhile the Sherpas had begun getting breakfast with a great deal of clattering and banging outside. We got up and put on our loden trousers and our down jackets. We turned our sleeping bags inside out and draped them over the roof of the tent, then shuffled in our down boots, over to the big mess tent.

Only about half of our team were in Base Camp. Some were up on the face fixing ropes between Camp I, which we had established at 6,000 metres, and Camp II which we hoped to set up at 6,600 metres. Ignazio Piussi had had to take our team doctor, Dr. Chierego, down to Dingpoche. Chierego, who had a practice in Verona, had succumbed to pulmonary oedema, a high altitude lung disorder, and had later to be flown out to Katmandu by helicopter. The loss of the expedition doctor had been a serious blow. To attempt such a major face without a doctor was a risky business, but what else could we do? We thought about having a new doctor flown in from Italy, but that would have taken too long. By the time one of us had got down to Katmandu, telephoned home and the CAI in Milan had found a suitable replacement, ten days at least would have gone by. Add to this the journey and the march-in – it would have been much too late. So we had to make do. Franco Guggiati, who was employed in a health insurance office back home, was put in charge of our medical supervision. And a very good job he made of it.

Aldo Anghileri's lean face was very sunburnt. Only for a moment as he greeted his friends at the breakfast table, did the sadness leave his eyes. There were still some people missing. We were waiting for Cassin, the leader, whom we fondly called 'the Old Man'. Aldo was a very close friend of his.

"What! Out of your sleeping bag already?" someone greets our leader.

"I don't know how you manage to get out of your narrow sleeping bag in the mornings with a hard-on like yours!"

Ribald laughter.

At the long tables some were eating hot rice cereal; Mario Curnis, a blond farmer from Bergamo, cut himself some ham and cheese. Cassin sat next to Anghileri and Leviti, to their right were the two Alippis – Giuseppe, known as Det, and Gigi Alippi – not related, but both from Lecco. Arcari sat on the end as he was usually the last to appear. Franco Guggiati in his new role as doctor was standing up doling out medicines with considerable dignity and circumspection.

They were all good climbers, amongst the best in Italy. There was scarcely an alpine climb that one or other of our 14-man team had not done. They all knew how things were going with us and what our chances were, but avoided open-speculation.

Every one of them was quite capable of climbing a vertical rock-face for days on end, sleeping in a hammock strung to the rock and hammering in pitons all the way from bottom to top. Now they were beginning to learn what it meant to face difficulties in rarefied air, that an expedition means more than just climbing, bivouacking and banging in pegs.

Most of them had already survived critical situations – bad falls, extreme cold with its attendant loss of feeling and the like – hopeless situations from which it seemed a miracle that they came through. Five or six had lost one or more climbing partners; some indeed had been written off themselves and had come back against all odds, like Gigi Alippi from the South Face of Mt. McKinley, Ignazio Piussi from the North-west Face of the Punta Tissi, to say nothing of Cassin himself, who has been climbing the most extreme of climbs for over forty years. Each time, however, they had behaved as if nothing unusual had happened, nothing for a climber to make a fuss about, and certainly

14

The Italian team at Lhotse Base Camp. *Standing from left to right:* Mario Curnis, Riccardo Cassin, Reinhold Messner, Alessandro Gogna, Ignazio Piussi, Det Alippi, Fausto Lorenzi, Franco Guggiati. *Kneeling:* Gigi Alippi, Aldo Leviti, Mario Conti, Gianni Arcari, Sereno Barbacetto. *Background:* the left part of the great ice ramp.

nothing to make one think of giving up climbing. Not on your life! They each cherished particular ambitions which they hoped yet to achieve, come what may. But they were not without fear. Fear is always a factor – fear in the night before a summit bid, fear in a blizzard, fear of one's own weakness and fear in the face of truly hopeless situations. However, the team as a whole behaved as if there was no such thing as fear, as though there were no reason for it at all. It just wasn't done to moan and complain; the danger was accepted as an intrinsic part of the game. And it was we ourselves who set out and maintained these unwritten taboos. With marked shows of indifference, we concealed our own insecurities and fear from the others, and in turn drew strength from their similar attitude.

Breakfast usually consisted of tea, marmalade and hard black peasant bread, which Riccardo Cassin had bought at home in the Aosta Valley. During this meal Aldo refrained from talking of his problems. After breakfast – we had in the meantime sorted out the loads for our

15

high altitude porters to take up the face – I went back to our tent. As I got my things together I noticed that Aldo was writing in his diary again. He had come to the decision that rather than play the hero here, it took far more courage and discipline to lead a normal civilian life, to work eight hours a day for a standard salary, to support a family and cope with all the everyday problems. He may have come to this conclusion in an attempt to rationalise his desire to go home, or he may have been truly convinced that a big expedition like ours made no sense at all. He himself certainly felt no further motivation in attempting such a face. "If it were two men against an eight-thousander", he said. "Now that would be a real challenge."

I nodded.

"I am thinking of my children and I reproach myself for my neglect of them", wrote Aldo in his diary. *"I have seldom given any real thought to what it means to be a father. I will do much more when I get home – it will all be very different. And I will take more time to be with you too, dear Mariella, for even if it seems that in the past I have never properly understood you because I was always off searching for new adventures and experiences, you are and will always be more important to me than the mountains.*

"On our march-in to Base Camp we met a solitary Hippy in the lower villages, and went along with him for a bit, chatting. It emerged that he had been on the road for five years; now and again he had taken hashish. For a few hours, he said, the drug brought a kind of release, but it wasn't important to him. There were some amongst us who couldn't accept his attitude and said he was a degenerate, others who said that at the very least he was irresponsible, but on me he made a good impression. After all, he had come as far as Dingpoche, 4,300 metres up, and had resolved to get to Everest Base Camp. Are not we climbers very much like this Hippy? Don't we seek a similar release through our climbing? Why else should we feel lost and miserable when we are not able to get out into the mountains. I can see little difference between the climber and the Hippy. We break away in search of some adventure or another, some mountain to climb, in order to get away from our everyday routine. Climbing is our escape, the particular drug that we seem to need.

"But at the same time climbing is a sport, and in my opinion just a sport. Whoever believes that he comes back from the mountain purer in soul and in some way uplifted, deludes himself. It is a fine distinction and I must confess to having difficulty in resolving it. One half of me wants to be Anghileri the Mountaineer, to prove myself and get up this damned mountain, but in another part of my mind, I feel that this face isn't so important, it's not the end of the world. The longer I stay on this immensely dangerous mountain side, time is ticking away, time I might be spending at home. These thoughts torment me, they are tearing me apart. The daily hazards and the distance that

16

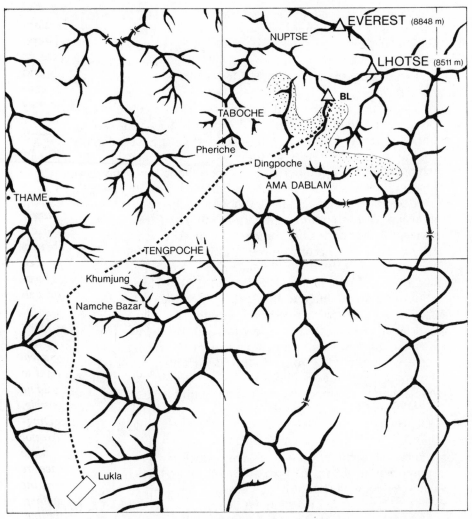

---------------- = Approach route of the Lhotse South Face Expedition, 1975
BL = Base Camp.

separates me from my wife and children are more than I can bear. The price is too high whether it be for a romantic ideal or a purely sporting challenge."

By now it was afternoon. According to the mid-day radio link-up, everything was all right on the face. Two men, Gogna and Barbacetto, had come back down to Base. They would be replaced the next day. For an hour I had been sitting on a large slab of gneiss between the tents and making some adjustments to my Titan crampons. Cassin had had these specially lightweight 12-pointers made for this expedition.

17

They were to be used for the final summit attempt. I had tried them out earlier and found them to be as light as a feather but a trifle unsteady. Whenever I put my whole weight over the front points, they wobbled badly. This was perhaps only because I wasn't used to them, but I had given up using them on the triple-boots for the time being in favour of my old ones.

Whenever the sun went behind the clouds it was bitterly cold. Shadows scuttled backwards and forwards across the face and a few minutes after 2 o'clock a powder-snow avalanche started in the narrow couloir separating the twin summits of the mountain. Like a small white cloud it swept down the face for about a thousand metres, then plunging over a dark overhang, it billowed out into space like a vast inside-out parachute and floated down, trailing a thin white plume in its wake. Only then did we hear the rattle and crashing of the falling rocks and the roar of the compressed air. The snow cloud continued falling for several seconds more, and it was many minutes before the last traces had settled and the snow slide which had been generated, had flowed down and vanished into the bergschrund. Quiet reigned once more on the huge wall. I had to crane my neck around to see up the 3,500 metre vertical wall to the summit. The upper half consisted of dark rock, criss-crossed by fine white veins, the lower section of rock ribs, ice cascades and smutty-grey runnels left by falling rocks. It seemed simply crazy to even consider climbing a direct line to the summit; for an expedition such as ours it was total madness. Avalanches and stonefalls, sometimes with blocks as large as houses, came down hourly. A 'direttissima' would take half a year and require at least eight intermediate camps – each of us would need to climb up and down ten times or more.

Fortunately there was a great ramp which ran from the left up to the summit ridge. In truth it was difficult enough and we didn't know what lay above it, but at least it was a little safer, relatively.

So far we had not made much height, but we still had at least four weeks in front of us. The Monsoon would not come until May at the earliest; by then we must have climbed our mountain or pulled out.

I went back into the tent. Aldo passed me the whisky bottle which he usually kept hidden in his personal belongings. Alessandro Gogna, who had joined Aldo, also took a gulp. Sandro, as we called him, still red in the face from his rapid descent down the wall, is well-known in climbing circles for the first solo ascent of the Walker Spur, the Badile Face in winter and so forth. Generally speaking he was a complete contrast to Aldo – tall and thin, lean-faced, large-nosed, and with a shock of black curls. He looked well; only his eyes had changed since our student days. Now they often had a glazed look about them and darted quickly back and forth. He was a nervous type, this Sandro. He

Alessandro Gogna, one of the most active of young Italian climbers.

said himself that he often felt he had a split personality, but when it came to climbing, he knew exactly where he was. It was this that gave him his ambition and subconsciously he realised this. We had known each other a long time but never before been together on a climb. I had always had an uneasy feeling that I wouldn't want to depend on him completely. Sandro was 30 years old, had been married for several years, and he burned with an ambition that he would neither acknowledge to himself nor to others. Aldo and he were old friends and I had shared a tent with them for a week. The two had made a first ascent together in the Brenta and were quick to spring to each other's defence if their honour as climbers was questioned. Sandro and Aldo understood each other without having to say very much. In some things they felt alike. Sandro knew all about Aldo's problems; they had talked them over before I was even aware of them. Now Aldo read to both of us what he had written during the course of the afternoon, as much to clarify it in his own mind as anything else:

"I am not going to let myself get embroiled in what amounts to no more or less than a direct prize fight again. No more expeditions. Certainly no more big expeditions like this. Only with one or two friends would I consider anything like this again."

In Base Camp there was almost nothing to do. The cooking was taken care of by the Sherpas, and the preparation of the loads which had to be sent day by day up the Face, took at most an hour in the morning. Every two or three days local porters brought up wood from the valley and the Sherpas took it in turns to ferry supplies from Base Camp to the higher camps, as we did in reconnoitring and fixing ropes on the face. So I spent most of the time that I was in Base Camp just reading in my tent or chatting with my friends.

Aldo had finally resolved to leave the expedition and go home. He had thought a lot about what people would say, those who expected him to return as a conqueror and his climbing friends in Lecco. How would they judge him? Many of them had been envious of his invitation to take part in the expedition. But for all this, it had to be his own decision and he was convinced that he must follow his own feelings in the matter and take the consequences for them. If he was to end his unhappiness, he must ignore the views and criticisms of others. It was his own life. He had reached the pitch where he felt that only flight, only withdrawal from the expedition, could restore his balance of mind. Once home, he was convinced, his wife and children would help him back onto an even keel. He would certainly want to climb again, as he had done for fifteen years. But in the Alps, never more than two or three days from home, where there were climbs enough, both easy and difficult, to satisfy his time and desire, and whatever conditions prevailed. He hadn't got the temperament to sit around in Base Camp for weeks nor to fix ropes for days on end.

"All this waiting about in Base Camp, all the climbing on jumars day after day has become a nightmare to me", said Aldo sadly.

"That's a necessary part of an expedition of this kind."

"But it's not climbing, it's just hard work that I have to force myself to do."

Towards evening the wind on the ridge dropped almost completely. Instead of the kilometre-long snow plume, grey clouds shrouded the summit, their southern edges pale and indistinct. The rumble of avalanches had replaced the usual howling of the wind. Sandro and I discussed at length what we ought to do next, and I promised to go up the face again the following morning.

"It's time we got cracking and established Camp II."

"Yes, if the weather holds, that's what you should do."

"The snow ridge, from the rock spur to the camp, is it safe?"

"Partly."

"Partly – Christ! What do you mean partly?"

"Well to the left there seems to be an icefall and to the right it keeps breaking away."

20

"Much?"

"Oh, yes – I've never seen such a place, great slices drop off every minute!"

"Apart from that, is the route safe?"

"There's a deep gully to the right which swallows everything that comes down. It remains to be seen what there is to the left."

"I'll find that out the day after tomorrow."

That ended the discussion.

"Goodnight!"

"Sleep well!"

I kept turning this conversation over in my mind, trying to imagine the way ahead. We were still 200 metres short of the great ice ramp which bisects the left half of the Lhotse Face diagonally from bottom right to upper left. In the middle the ramp was joined by our spur. The question was, did a safe bridge exist between the two, or had all our efforts to date been in vain?

An unusual stillness prevented me from sleeping; I felt as if my ears were stuffed with cotton wool. It seemed hardly possible that the storm had simply died out and that several hours had gone by without a single avalanche coming down. Next morning the face was only visible through a veil of grey mist. It was as if the whole basin below the South Face had been filled with little clouds. The sky was only visible now and again when the clouds parted.

"A thick bank of mist, but probably clear above", I suggested at breakfast.

"No – the weather forecast is lousy."

"You can't rely on that – it's always wrong". I was annoyed by Sandro's report.

"It could have stayed fine for two days for Christ's sake. At this rate we're never going to get any further."

I stayed in Base Camp and the others who were up on the face, all came down. Around midday heavy clouds again moved in over Lhotse. They were especially thick around Island Peak and it looked as if a new cloud front was sweeping in from the south and would envelop us in a few hours. The lower part of the 3,500 metre face loomed over us, unbelievably steep, sombre and awesome. The wind when it buffeted its slabs and buttresses, bellowed like a raging sea; the whole rock-face had the appearance of being in perpetual motion. The upper slopes, which were hidden from view, spewed down stones and chunks of ice and avalanches. It was uncanny.

The next morning Aldo spoke to Riccardo Cassin about his decision. Sandro and I were there. There was no fuss. Although Riccardo took it as a personal affront that one of his team should want to quit, he did

21

Aldo Anghileri with his two children.

his best to understand what Aldo was going through, and Aldo certainly put his case over well. Cassin asked us what we thought and we agreed that in the circumstances Aldo should be allowed to go. Riccardo tried his best to dissuade him. He promised him light duties, he could stay in Base Camp and need not go up the face again. There was always plenty to do lower down; Base Camp personnel were just as important to an expedition as the climbing team. But Aldo would have nothing to do with such a compromise. Either he was a climber as he had intended, went up the face and maybe made a summit attempt if called upon to do so, or he went home. He didn't want to stick around in Base Camp, he had had enough. He wanted out, Basta!

SO MUCH EFFORT
FOR A FEW METRES

We were only a few rope-lengths from a plateau, but I could scarcely make it out through the drifting snow. Mario Curnis had installed himself in a narrow ice crack and was belaying me whilst I traversed out westwards across the snow-covered ice. For one brief moment the mists parted and I could see right down to the foot of the mountain. 1,600 metres below. The rock fell away almost vertically beneath me. There was sunlight down there, a bright patch of it, and warmth. Up here I was only managing about ten metres before I had to stop and catch my breath. Breaking the trail was such strenuous work; the loose snow was not only tiring it also required extra caution.

I moved my right foot and I heard a sound, a short, sharp, ominous crack. My movement had caused the crust covering the snow to cave in. It seemed to shudder and I expected it all to come away; quickly I jammed in my iceaxe and clung onto it with both hands, but nothing happened.

Whenever I rested, I wiggled my toes, pressing them first hard down in my boots, then up against the toe-caps. This was to keep my circulation going and to ensure that none of my digits went numb. On Nanga Parbat in 1970 I had been badly frostbitten and I was now particularly susceptible to cold. I had to take extra precautions, I couldn't afford to get frostbitten again. As the feeling crept back into my feet, they first tingled, then throbbed painfully. The stumps of my amputated toes felt on fire, but I didn't mind the pain for at least it meant that blood was still circulating and my toes were not in imminent danger.

The snow had continued drifting and as I rested, little piles of it were building up on my gloves and my beard was caked in it. I could no longer see the small plateau ahead and was thus having difficulty finding the route. It was most important that I didn't stray too far to the left because of the danger of falling ice.

If I looked hard, I could just see the motionless figure of Mario directly below me, but it was impossible to tell whether or not he was still looking after the rope. I was happy to leave myself in his hands.

"Sure – he'll be belaying me all right." I didn't bother my head any

23

more about what he was doing on his windy stance but edged forward once more another ten steps. I focused my whole attention and will-power onto the single spot which we must reach this afternoon.

A gust of wind delivered a sentence to me as clearly as if the words had been spoken just a few metres away.

"Where are you?"

Mario's voice sounded dry and uncertain. My position was too precarious to answer him right away. An awkward move of my head could easily have thrown me off balance. Gingerly I took a few more steps upwards, testing each carefully with my axe and crampons. The snow cover was some 30 or 40 centimetres thick; as I stepped onto it, my feet sank through and wallowed a bit before my crampons gripped firm ice underneath. At last I could stop comfortably. I shouted down to Mario.

"There's another 50 metres to go. Can you give me all the slack you've got!"

"O.K. Understood."

His voice, whilst not exactly cheerful, sounded a shade brighter. The layer of snow on my clothing had grown thicker and thicker while I was stopped, and now encased me like armour-plating. Every time I moved bits and pieces broke off and hundreds of little ice-balls were left dangling from my arms and legs.

With the increase in height, the wind had gained in intensity. I glanced at my altimeter, which I wore on a string round my neck under my pullover. "Another 50 metres", I thought, "Another 50 metres and I should be at 6,600 metres. By then I should have reached the great ramp. Then I'll be able to come down. We'll have done what we set out to do."

At that moment it didn't occur to me that an altimeter registers higher in bad weather than is actually the case, but I kept on hoping that one good run-out would see me to a site suitable for Camp II. The wall above appeared to steepen. The 200 metre climbing rope hung from my harness like a leaden tail. I could only take at most ten steps between rests, the muscles in the tops of my thighs ached so.

At last I was standing on the small saddle which linked our ridge with the great ramp. To the right was the avalanche gully Sandro was telling me about three days before, but by keeping to the left I came to the foot of a slab which formed part of the ramp. Success! This encouraged me no end and gave me fresh strength.

I now started looking for a suitable campsite. The top layer of snow had been blown away by the wind, and I sank up to my ankles in the soft under snow. I was glad when half an hour later I reached a mirror-smooth ice wall, up which I could make some progress. It was less strenuous than the floundering steps I had been taking, but it did require total concentration. It would be so easy to slip on this hard, brittle ice.

I now stood a good 150 metres above Mario. I had placed two intermediate belays – long ice pitons. It was a long pitch. At last I was able to put in an ice-screw. At every step I could feel the weight of the rope tugging at my chest, teasing me off balance. What a sweat! In the middle of the ice wall I put in my second ice-screw and felt a bit more secure. I somehow felt that because of the unusually long run-out between Mario and me, it would be relatively easy to arrest a fall. Towards the top of the blue-green ice shield I chiselled out another little hole in the glassy surface, put in a further screw and turned it with the pick of my axe, turn after turn, until the ring was flush with the ice.

Only now could I think out my moves for the next few metres. It was the kind of situation everyone dreads. Crusted snow on top of blank ice. Each step spelt danger. There was a hollow between the snow and ice, so that whenever I failed to get the points of my crampons right through the crust to the smooth ice underneath, I was threatened with slipping right off. It was just as if someone was trying to pull the ground from under my feet. It was gradually getting brighter and I tried by means of signs to let Mario know of my dangerous situation.

In response he oscillated the rope so that I could more easily draw it up behind me. His efforts made it snake up to the first intermediate belay. Mario had certainly not been asleep, he had put as much concentration into this pitch as I had, and been just as aware of its hazards. He now tensed, assuming the hunched-up position a second man always adopts if he thinks his leader might come off. He was prepared for the worst, though naturally he hoped it wouldn't come to that.

Not until I had taken a few steps upwards and turned around to indicate that the crisis was over, did he relax. Then he straightened up and I could see him shuffling from one foot to the other impatiently. Suddenly he paused and began a systematic examination of the ice pegs to which he was secured, making sure they were all holding. He also checked the knots for he had tied them with his iced-up gloves on and he wanted to be sure they were OK. Apparently all was well.

I climbed up as far as the first terrace, but no further. Not because I was convinced it was an ideal site for Camp II, but because it was time to descend. As usual when I reached a goal I had set myself, I could see the next place I wanted to aim at and had to force myself to turn around. I was tired, but not exhausted. Snow clung to my clothes and face but it didn't bother me. Nor did the wind; it was stronger now but not carrying so much new snow as before. There was a hollow where

25

the slope was quite flat. There was no avalanche cone beneath it and a few crevasses above. I recognised it as the first possible site for the new camp. With that I resolved to go down. I rammed my axe firmly in, untied myself and fastened the end of the rope to the axe. Quickly I attached a length of line to my harness, made a loop and clipped in a karabiner. Then clipping in to the fixed rope also, I at once began the descent. To the ice screws that I had inserted on the way up, I attached the rope with a clove hitch climbing down always on the main rope.

Without stopping, I abseiled down the dangerous avalanche slopes and plunged through the new snow back to Mario.

He was apparently suffering from the cold, and to keep his circulation going, was doing little exercises with his hands and feet. He would kick the toes of his boots repeatedly against the ice wall and clap his fists together. Finally he tried to find some food, normally an easy job but a bit tricky here on his airy perch. He rummaged in his rucksack and came out with some frozen dried fruit and a piece of chocolate. He handed some across to me in his snowy gloves. The sticky prunes were coated in snow as we stuffed them into our mouths.

Mario was very cold and therefore keen to get going, but was obviously pleased with the results of our reconnaissance. We clipped all the spare pitons and karabiners from our belts onto one of the belaying pitons, where we would be certain to find them again on a future climb.

"Now", I said "down we go!"

But Mario hesitated before clamping his jumar to the rope. As is usual with exertion at this altitude, he was breathing through his mouth, and his short breaths quickly condensed and hung like clouds between us.

"We mustn't follow too closely. Each peg will only take the weight of one of us", Mario said. He spoke in a slow monotone.

"You're right", I said and began the descent of the snow-encrusted rope.

During the next two hours we abseiled down as fast as we could. Over knife-sharp ridges, overhanging ice, vertical rock steps. Every so often the first man repeated the gymnastic exercises to keep warm, while the other slid rapidly down the fixed ropes. It was the only way to fight the cold. We were hoping that we could get some hot soup or tea at Camp I to quench our thirst. There must surely be a few Sherpas there. Perhaps they were expecting us.

We had to be continually on our guard to prevent an unforeseen accident. We warned each other whenever we approached a particularly dangerous spot. Our situation was not critical, but it was serious.

The cloud had risen, for which we were thankful. During a breather above the great rock buttress, I suggested to Mario that I thought we should tackle the rest of the descent and not stay on in Camp I. He didn't say a word, he had lost the inclination to make decisions.

Over and over again during my 25 years as a climber, I have found myself face to face with unavoidable danger. I began to think of similar serious situations I had been in and how they could turn in an instant into a battle for survival. Death isn't something you dwell on, but all too suddenly it can stare you in the face as a very real possibility. I could sense it quite clearly now and knew that evasive action had to be taken promptly to avert disaster. A moment's carelessness could be fatal. The rock was all iced up, snow clung in all the cracks and gullies and lay knee-deep on the slabs and projections. And this snow slid away under our feet in small avalanches as we gingerly felt our way down the convex face.

Mario could see the position as well as I. He was still wearing his crampons, even though their points kept getting caught in snow-filled cracks. This was very dangerous and he could easily have overbalanced and fallen backwards down the face. Luckily there were fixed ropes all the way from where we had turned back. A free climb here, even for the best of climbers, would be quite out of the question.

Wet and dangerously chilled as we were, we dared not remain in the first high camp. The three hour descent had taken its toll. We were not only soaked through but also tired out. This bad weather might last a week. We must – like it or not – get on down to Base Camp.

We stayed half an hour only in Camp I to have a drink and a chat with our friends and the Sherpas. We gulped tea and poured gallons of fizzy drink down our throats, but it was not enough. What wouldn't we give to rid ourselves of this terrible thirst! We had to get going if we wanted to get down the 700 metres to base in daylight. Mario drank the last drip of melted ice and gave the mug back to the Sherpa in the cook tent.

"Remember us to everyone at Base Camp", cried one of the Sahibs from his tent as we clipped into the fixed ropes, "and tell the Old Man to send us up a couple of Sherpa girls!"

We took hold of the fixed rope and began our abseil.

"Washed, and by air mail!" grinned Mario as he slid off into the void.

CAMP II AT LAST

Three days later on April 13th we continued our work on the face. I had only stayed one day in Base Camp before coming up again with Aldo Leviti to erect the second high camp. Now both camps were occupied. There were a few Sahibs and half a dozen Sherpas in Camp I, and Leviti and I in Camp II.

Leviti was the Benjamin of our party, barely 25 years old, a ski and climbing instructor with the Italian Customs Service. Most of his mountaineering experience had been gained in the Dolomites, where he had done a large number of the very hardest climbs. He had taken part in the Italian Mammut Expedition to Everest in 1973, but could not really be said to be experienced in expedition work. Some of his remarks about our route and tactics displayed a certain naivety. He was small-built, very quick and strong, and had a seemingly inexhaustible fund of ribald stories with which he kept us amused. In the face of danger he didn't lack courage and determination.

Muffled to the ears, Leviti got the radio out of his sleeping bag and waited for the call sign. Dead on 6 o'clock Cassin's voice came through:

"Base Camp calling Camp I, come in please."

There was a lot of crackling and whistling and we couldn't catch the rest of the conversation. Then:

"Understood", that was Cassin again. It was the communications between Camps I and II that were bad, obviously, for we could hear Cassin clearly enough.

"Base Camp calling Camp II".

"Camp II to Base, can you hear us?"

"Very well."

"We've found a good site up here, at about 6,600 metres, it's fairly safe."

"What do you mean – fairly safe?"

"Well, there are two big crevasses just above us and they swallow most of the stuff that comes down. Of course if half of the Ramp broke away, we should have had it. But it's the best site anywhere round here."

"What will you do tomorrow?"

"We'll go on climbing."

"The weather forecast's bad. There's a storm brewing."

"That's all we need! What's new down there?"

"Anghileri left today. Piussi and the two Alippi's are working on the cable lift."

"That's great. Until tomorrow, then. Goodnight to you all."

The wind came in great gusts, it was so strong we had the feeling it might carry us away. I didn't open the tent door again until 10 o'clock the next morning. The blizzard, which had been raging all night, burst upon me with full force, threatening to rip the thin canvas out of my hands. Snow poured in the opening and it was only with great difficulty that I managed to close it up again. I sank back exhausted.

Gradually the storm abated and when it became quiet once more, I again tried to open the tent. A fresh squall struck me; it was just as if the storm had been lying in wait for my reappearance. Snow and hailstones caught me full in the face. But this time I was ready for it and grabbing my rolled up sleeping bag, I jammed it in the opening so that no more snow could come in. I waited for another lull, then quickly

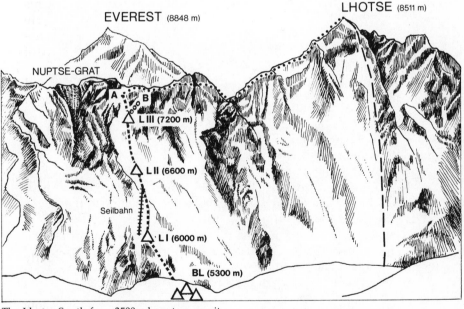

The Lhotse South face, 3500m base to summit.

•••••••••••• = Proposed route to summit.

■■■■■■■■■■■■■ = Italian route 1975.

— — — — — — = Direttissima.

BL = Base Camp.

A = Attempt by Gogna and Barbacetto.

B = Highest point reached by

Messner and Curnis.

29

opened the zip again and stepped outside, shutting the tent up behind me. The storm swallowed me up, howling and raging all about me, the wind whirling round the tent threatened to batter it to pieces. For a few moments I was completely engulfed in driving snow with the wind tearing at my clothes. I clung on to the ice-cold roof of the tent with one hand and my hat with the other. Then I tottered a few steps from the tent entrance, cut two small steps in the snow, and stood in them.

The wind up here at Camp II was particularly violent, but every now and again there was a lull. I began to enjoy struggling against the elements, standing there in my little steps and swallowing great draughts of cold air. I took stock of the situation. Up on the summit ridge, clouds and shreds of mist were scurrying about. Another squall. Another lull. Our camp in a hollow of the mountain was completely covered in snow, all our tents, ice-axes, other equipment. The swirling wind poked snow into every cranny.

"You seem to like it out there", came Leviti's voice from inside the tent.

"It's not so bad."

A few minutes later, the tent door opened a crack and Leviti peered out.

"Once you get used to it", I said "It's O.K. It sounds far worse from in there."

"Well, I'll have to come out – my bladder's bursting!" And with these words, Leviti pulled down the zip and stepped out.

"We'll stay put today", I said. "Rest a bit and conserve our energy. The next five or six hundred metres don't look so bad. We could do them even in bad weather. We'll have a go tomorrow."

By now Leviti had joined me. He was stiff after the long night cramped in the tent, and as he struggled against the force of the wind, he tottered uncertainly like a sick, old man. He screwed up his eyes against the bright light and his forehead was furrowed by deep wrinkles. He muttered disconsolately that he would prefer to get on with the climb than sit around in the tent all day just listening to the gale.

As was usual around 10 o'clock, the weather began to worsen. It wasn't just the wind we had to contend with now, it was cloud as well. The bank of mist that had filled the valleys, was climbing higher and becoming much thicker, threatening to envelop everything and those clouds over the ridge which only a short while ago had been so wispy, were building up into an impenetrable mass. The gale slowly subsided and by the afternoon it had begun to snow heavily.

Leviti began to write in his diary and I to read one of the books I had brought up with me. In this way I tried not to think of the avalanche danger which was increasing with every hour the snow kept falling.

But however obstinately I tried to persuade myself there was nothing to worry about, I couldn't concentrate on the book. Suddenly I realised I hadn't taken in a word of it and I tossed it aside.

During the evening Leviti tried desperately to make contact with Base Camp, and although conditions were very bad, his persistence eventually paid off and he heard a thin voice coming over the air. The weather forecast was still the same, we learned, and if conditions didn't ease up, we were to climb down the next day. However, the storm was expected to abate during the night, if one was to believe the Nepalese Weather Centre. The temperature was falling and the advance of a high pressure zone from the West suggested that the bad weather would pass over in two or three days at most.

"My nerves won't stand another two or three sleepless nights in this storm", said Leviti.

"If we can't climb any higher tomorrow, then we'll go back to Base Camp", I promised.

While we were pinned down on the mountain, Aldo Anghileri was sauntering along through the rhododendron forest between the Monastery of Tengpoche and Namche Bazar. He was all by himself; travelling so light, he didn't need a porter. Anghileri hadn't had any qualms about saying farewell to us, but now he was overwhelmed with a singular feeling of loneliness. His thoughts went out to Fausto Lorenzi and Mario Curnis who were just leaving for Camp I as he came away; he had wished them luck as he shook hands, and now they must already be well up on the face. Looking back, he could see the long black line of the Lhotse Wall. Higher up where the storm boiled, that must be where Camp II was situated. What did it feel like to be up there, he wondered, trying to find the way ahead. For the first time he felt apart from it all, he no longer belonged to the expedition and was beset with a feeling of unworthiness, failure almost. Where was Sandro now? Sandro, who had been so moved when he said goodbye, that Aldo had come close to tears himself.

"Sandro felt the same as I did", he thought "but he stayed on." And then:

"Will he make it? I hope so, for his sake. He needs an eight-thousander."

When he left, he had wanted Sandro to come with him, but now with all his heart, he hoped his friend would stick it out to the end. Sandro was a good friend, the only person on the expedition he felt at ease with. On a boulder close to Base Camp, Sandro had stood a long time watching Aldo pick his way over the grey boulders of the moraine, down to the valley. They had kept waving to each other.

31

Sandro! Aldo felt he understood him now. All those conflicts which raged within him and gave him that feeling of a divided personality. But didn't Sandro make it worse for himself by suppressing his instincts and forcing himself to climb against his will? Aldo thought about the book Sandro had written. It was full of contradictions and had been much discussed in Base Camp. He thought now he could see what Sandro was trying to say. But why, if he really felt all those things he wrote, hadn't he also pulled out from the expedition?

"These accursed mountains! This bloody face!" He barely refrained from crying the words aloud.

The luxurious sweetness of the rhododendrons enveloped him, every bit as completely as had the storm a few days before.

Then in an instant Aldo saw everything with stark clarity. What a good thing he had had the courage to make the final break! If the others wanted to toil and slave up there, that was their look out, but he, he would soon be home.

Over the radio I had asked Aldo to call my wife when he got back. Perhaps he would see her at the Mountain Film Festival in Trento and would be able to tell her how we were getting on. He knew that she was proposing to come out to Nepal herself, with her sister and a friend, to visit me in Base Camp.

It was late in the morning when I placed the fixed rope in position at the top of a steep snow slope and with my sleeve, tried to brush the icicles from my beard. In three hours we hadn't made 300 metres of height. The gale was still raging with undiminished fury as it had for days. "That's enough for today, come on down! shouted Leviti, who was standing up to his waist in snow on a somewhat flatter surface. The appearance of the Ramp had altered dramatically in the last two days. Instead of the shimmering patches of blue ice, interspersed with ribs and ridges, there was now, as far as you could see through half-closed eyes, a billowing chaos, a formless confusion of tumbled white blocks, white mist and swirling white snow. The horizon had vanished. The storm had fashioned a completely new world out of the old. There were no tracks or landmarks, nothing to see but the boiling snow.

"Come on! Let's get down to Base Camp."

"Right. There's nothing to gain up here."

Once we had reached the flatter ground near Camp II, where the snow lay deep, we floundered about, struggling in vain to make some steady headway. Leviti was in front of me, he was wading through the drifts, his trunk swaying from side to side. At times it seemed he would collapse under the snow altogether.

The South Face of Lhotse (8511 m) is 3500 m from the foot of the wall to the summit and is one of the highest and most difficult walls in the world. The lower part is longer, steeper and more difficult than the Eigerwand. The upper section twice the length of the N. Face of The Cima Grande. The original objective, the 'Direttissima' runs up the buttress in the summit fall line. A problem for the year 2000.

"And all for nothing!" I thought. "Three days we've held out against this storm and we have barely 100 metres to show for it."

It was only thinking about Uschi, my wife, that kept me going during that dreadful descent. In a month or less she would be here, and by then too, we should know if we had won or lost with this mountain. It didn't seem important any more whether we reached the summit or not. She was all that mattered now. I wondered what she was doing at this minute? Whether she had received my letters? Whether Anghileri would get in touch with her?

As I roped down, I peered through the mist trying to make out the features of the mountain, the slabs and cracks and crevices, the footholds I needed. Nowhere was there a dry spot. Perhaps one of the ropes had frayed? Perhaps more? It was impossible to tell under their thick grey coating of ice and there was not time to check each length.

"They'll be O.K.", we told ourselves.

Just below Camp I we met a party coming up, led by Sereno Barbacetto, a tough climber from Bolzano, and Sandro Gogna. They were on their way to Camp II. Sandro wanted to know what the route was like. Sereno, a somewhat eccentric character, stood by but said nothing.

"What's the Ramp like?"

"To begin with – easy, but there's masses of snow, we could hardly see a thing."

"Any ropes up there?"

"Yes, one."

"Pegs?"

"Half a dozen, hanging on the axe I used to attach the fixed rope to. But pegs and screws aren't much good up there. What you need is dead-men.* Tell the Sherpas to bring up some bits of wood; you can make your own out of curved pieces. Bury them knee-deep in the snow and fix the rope to them!"

Meanwhile Barbacetto had climbed on. He liked to climb alone. He had soloed such great routes as the Ortler North Face, the French Buttress on the Crozzon di Brenta, and several routes on the Croz dell'Altissimo. It was I who had suggested him for this expedition, but now I wondered if I had been right. He was a brilliant climber, strong and careful, but he was a loner. He would, as I suppose I had known all along, always prefer to climb solo and found it difficult to fit in with a team.

"Best of luck!" Sandro went after him.

Half an hour later we were back in Base Camp, soaked to the skin.

*Dead-man – usually a small alloy plate, which is dug into the snow. The harder it is pulled, the deeper it digs into the snow, like the fluke of an anchor.

THE AVALANCHE DISASTER

I now occupied a tent on my own. It was pitched on a natural platform above the equipment store, higher than the rest of the camp and closer to the face.

I slept soundly, no longer plagued by those dreadful, endless fantasies which so often tear the night to shreds after a strenuous day. Tonight, however, I did dream:

I was earnestly negotiating with a farmer from my own village over the price he wanted for his farm. Together we inspected the barns, the wood and the fields. The sun was already low into the notch between the Tschann and the Rittner Horn by the time we came to an agreement, which we sealed with a firm handshake. It had been my life's ambition to own a farm of my own and I was so delighted with the prospect that I put my arms round the farmer's wife, kissed her and held her close. Uschi, who had been following these proceedings with interest, now kissed the farmer. In my dream this behaviour didn't seem in any way unusual. We were brimful with happiness.

I had no idea what happened next. From my dream of green meadows, I awoke fighting for my life. The tent had disappeared, I was in the centre of a whirlwind. Snow and storm raged around me. I fought to draw breath and I could no longer tell which way up I was. I was just part of a terrible roaring and crashing as if the world was being rent into pieces. Then I was completely engulfed and it seemed as if all life would be crushed out of me. I knew I had to struggle, had to swim with my arms if I was to have any chance of getting to the surface. All this took but an instant, but I knew instinctively what had happened. It was no supernatural phenomenon, on the contrary something all too natural. An avalanche had hit Base Camp and soon all would be over.

Blocks of ice – or were they oxygen cylinders? – flew past me. I ducked and made more swimming motions with my outstretched arms. I couldn't tell if it was me that was moving or if everything around me was rolling and tumbling about. Was I still in the same place? Certainly the tent was no longer above me, but my feet were still in my sleeping bag. Without remembering how and when I awoke,

35

I must have come to my senses the minute the first clouds of snow roared over Base Camp. I suspected that we had only caught the air turbulence stirred up by the avalanche, otherwise I should surely not have been spared to tell the tale. Panic had gripped me for a few seconds, but now that it was all over I felt surprisingly calm and dispassionate. As the blast subsided and the snow settled, I found myself sitting up to my waist in thick powder snow.

"This is a bloody shambles", I said to myself, "Now I must find another tent."

It was only then that I realised I was barefoot and dressed only in my underclothes. The air was still full of snow-dust and the usual night wind was blowing. I couldn't make out exactly where I was, nor could I find any boots or clothes. Were the other tents in front of me, or behind? Or to the other side, perhaps? Were there still any other tents even? Nothing moved – not a sound, no light, no sign of life at all, just the inky blackness. I began to tug my sleeping bag out of the jumbled snow, helped by the wind which whisked the blocks of ice all over the place and threatened to wrench the icy bag out of my hands altogether. I gathered it up into a bundle, jammed it under my left arm and barefooted, stumbled over the stony snow in the direction I felt the rest of the camp must be. The fine powder snow clung to my still warm feet; they were aching badly, but I couldn't tell whether they were hot or cold. I staggered about for a long time without finding anything. I felt devastatingly lost and alone. Then suddenly right below me, I spotted a light. It was the camp!

Nobody seemed unduly alarmed; one or two of the tents had suffered but none of them had been swept away completely like mine. The Sherpas didn't hang about for long and Cassin too, soon went back to his tent.

I crawled in with Mario Conti, a short dark-haired climber from Lecco, whom we called 'Mariolino' to distinguish him from Mario Curnis. He was very upset and took a while to calm down. He lent me some of his clothes and plucked the lumps of ice out of my hair.

"I'm not going to stay here another night longer."

"Me neither."

"Bloody place."

"We'll have to shift the whole Base Camp tomorrow."

"I've never been caught out like that before."

"It could have been a lot worse. We could have lost all the tents and everything; we might have been left with no clothes to put on and all the porters in a panic."

"It doesn't bear thinking about."

"Was it new snow that avalanched, do you think?"

"No, it must have been ice. There are great blocks of it lying about everywhere."

"Shouldn't we have foreseen that? Doesn't it mean we're too close to the face?"

"That's what I think. But lots of camps have used the same site before us."

"And we had to be the poor sods to cop it!"

"That's right."

"I'm not going to get caught like that again. I won't make that same mistake twice."

"Five expeditions have camped here on this spot – the Karwendel team in 1970 when they climbed Lhotse Shar, three Japanese parties and now us. The site has been used for ten years; just our luck to cop it now."

I suddenly remembered that my camera and the manuscript for my new book "Bergvölker", on which I had been making the final corrections, must both be buried in the snow. Mariolino and I got up and searched everywhere and we eventually found both of them under a jumble of boxes and clothes and lumps of ice. I felt a lot better.

The space between the tents was ankle-deep in powder snow with scraps of clothing and tents showing through the surface here and there. On the side nearest the mountain some of our tents had collapsed. By the light of our torches, it looked as if the whole camp had received a coat of whitewash. Everywhere the onrush of air pressure had met with no resistance, it had left in its wake a fluted surface, capillaries of ice, for all the world like varicose veins in the snow.

Mario Conti, although accustomed to the vicious Patagonian storms of Cerro Torre, couldn't get to sleep for a long time. What would happen if a bigger block of ice broke away from the wall? My dreams that night were all about learning to swim.

It was 5.30 in the morning and still icy cold. I had been dozing fitfully for half an hour, unable to erase the memory of the avalanche from my mind. I was thinking about our friends up on the face and wondering how they were faring, when suddenly, towards 6 o'clock, I sensed that something else threatened. "Another avalanche? Why now?" I wondered, "Why should a second avalanche strike now?" But Mariolino had also been woken by the muffled boom. It was followed by a droning that vibrated the whole tent for some seconds. Mariolino threw aside the down jacket which at night he used to spread over his sleeping bag, sat up and listened intently. He thought of the horrors of the previous evening – the blast of air pressure and the snow heaped up at the tent door. But everything was quiet again, it seemed peaceful

37

enough, yet we could not shake off the uneasy feeling that something menaced us. This conviction grew, tingling through us like an electric shock. And then quite clearly we could hear a mighty rumbling high above.

"What was that?" Mariolino cried, and a nervous demoniacal smile flickered across his face for an instant. Doubtfully he fumbled for a zip' of his sleeping bag.

"A second avalanche maybe", I said it half in earnest, half in jest, hoping it was not so. But a few more seconds confirmed our worst fears. The thundering came closer and closer. Mariolino made a leap for the tent entrance and tore the flaps apart. He gasped in terror as he saw in place of the Lhotse Face, just one mighty avalanche. The sky was filled with the seething turbulence, as high as the mountain, as high as he could see. Like an atomic mushroom the pulverised snow hung in the air. The sight of it froze him to the spot for a brief second, then he came to himself and I saw his features tighten, his eyes widen as he braced every muscle, every sinew, against the impending fury. I caught his intention and immediately took up a similar defensive attitude. We cowered together, heads bent low, the sleeping bags over our legs, and our hands spread out to ward off disaster.

At first only a slight tremor in the air, a vibration in the toes and fingers, and then something caught my breath away. In the same instant we were without a roof over our heads. Tentpoles whirled through the air, bits and pieces of clothing flew about and powder snow was forced into my nose and mouth. Only with difficulty could I open my eyes the tiniest crack. The whole scene was a repetition of last night's devastation. Again I paddled my arms and tried to clear my mouth. Instinctively we had both rolled over to take the full force of the avalanche on our backs. I couldn't tell whether it came from behind us or in front, or indeed whether it had stopped altogether. Was Mariolino still beside me or had he been swept away? What was that flying through the air? Was it a rock or a box? Oxygen cylinders sailed past like deep-water fish. Cartouches of gas, lumps of ice. Was I still in the same place or had I too been borne away by this grey-white flood? I shuddered to think.

A short pause, I breathed again. Over? Safe? Casting a quick glance round, I perceived that the dark shape behind me must be Mariolino; he was still swimming with his arms. I noticed that we were huddled in the same direction as the main flow of the avalanche, but in the next instant we were again caught up and whipped anew into wild confusion. For more than ten minutes we were crushed and buffeted and battered with ice and snow. But worst of all was the feeling that we were suffocating to death.

Then quite suddenly, the ordeal was over, leaving havoc in its wake.

My breath came in gulps, my pulse was hammering so loudly that it must surely be heard for miles around. Mariolino and I looked dumbly at each other, trying to take it all in. I spat out the snow. Mariolino's face was furrowed and worn. He was still covered in pressed snow; when he ran his hand through his hair, the snow clung in little lumps, like dung from a cow. We were both trembling all over.

There were no tents left standing. The food and equipment stores had been swept away and the expedition kitchen, which had originally been four dry-stone walls with a plastic sheet for a roof, had been reduced to a heap of rubble. It was a grim outlook. Where were the Sahibs? The Sherpas? Tschottre, our Liaison Officer? The tent belonging to Curnis and Lorenzi had gone and Cassin's lay as if it had been flattened by a steam roller. Mariolino was coughing. From the start he had not acclimatised well and suffered badly from the cold and damp. He would have been the ideal man for a summit party, quick and light, steady and experienced on most terrain. Now he just stood there a quivering wreck, completely demoralised. The gentle melancholy of his normal expression had given way to one of bitter disillusion. It was only when he saw signs of movement from the ruins of Cassin's tent that his eyes brightened and a raw smile crossed his face, indicating a glimmer of hope.

The yellow tent writhed and heaved like a dinosaur, rose, collapsed again, then finally stood erect. The zip fastener opened and out stepped 66-year old Riccardo Cassin, safe and sound. With commendable presence of mind, he had rescued the radio and now held it ready for reception. It was a few minutes after 6 o'clock, time for radio contact. Bow-legged, the Old Man stood there holding the receiver in his right hand and gesticulating at the mountain with his left, for all the world as if he were cursing it.

It was at this moment, looking up, that I first saw where the avalanche had come from. A massive block of ice – we reckoned it afterwards as something like a million cubic metres – had broken away from the face immediately beneath the site of our Camp II, and had swept down the couloir between the ramp and the ice spur. At about 6,600 metres, the couloir curves and this must have deflected the flow of the avalanche, from there immediately above us, it poured down the face and would have entombed us forever, had we not been camped on the moraine about 100 metres above the glacier. The steep moraine diverted the ice blocks to the left, averting the worst, but the avalanche blast alone had been sufficient to raze our Base Camp to the ground.

Our friends in Camps I and II had neither seen nor heard the avalanche. They thought Cassin was making a poor joke when he reported it over the radio.

39

"You're having us on!"

"No, it's serious – it looks frightful down here."

"Is anyone hurt?"

"All the Sahibs seem OK, but I can only see two Sherpas."

"This bloody mountain! Does this finish it?"

"We can't tell at the moment what the damage is."

While the Old Man continued describing our position, and gave the order for everyone to come back down to Base, we started digging for the missing Sherpas. We found one in the heap of rubble that had been our cookhouse about 20 metres below the camp. The Liaison Officer lay groaning under boxes of tinned food. It was a wonder that no-one was dead. The snow was stained with blood; one of the Sherpas was bleeding badly from the nose. After we had looked after the injured Sherpas – there were four in all – we sat down to rest and took stock of the situation. At first glance it looked as if there were no hope for the expedition. Our equipment lay scattered over three kilometres; 20 kilograms of heavy gas canisters had been hurled 60 metres into the valley below, but fortunately none of them had exploded. When a week later, we made a foray to the dead glacier below the mountain, we found all sorts of odds and ends strewn about – a gold purse with a few rupees in it, a photo of Conti's wife (quite a dish! a ski-instructress), a folding table from the mess tent, two letters and a card from Uschi. I hadn't missed them till then, although I keep everything she writes to me.

The Old Man kept shaking his head. He could see all his hopes and two year's work buried under ice and snow. Did it make any sense to go on? Four high-level Sherpas injured, half the equipment lost, and the team in very low spirits. We all assembled round the remaining gas-cooker for a conference; these get-togethers were a regular feature of the expedition, they had become quite a ritual. The Old Man always called a pow-wow if there were any basic decisions to be made. The future of the expedition would be decided in a similarly democratic fashion. We were still haunted by memories of the catastrophe. We still seemed to hear the cries of terror, picture the chaos, and feel ourselves stifling to death. Our friends, who had come down from the high camps, were even more surprised than we that no-one had been killed. Even so, having not experienced the event, they didn't view it in quite the same light as us. The five of us who had been in our tents when the avalanche struck didn't have much to say, but just sat resignedly by. We were like a circle of broken warriors, not beaten but chastened by the Gods.

*   *   *

The Sherpas had a simple explanation for our misfortune; we had killed a yak and as a result, at least one of us must die. The avalanches had been warnings merely of what the Gods had in store for us. Angtsering, the Sirdar, and Tschottre, the Liaison Officer, both begged us to abandon the expedition. This belief in the wrath of the Gods wasn't just superstition, they claimed, they had proof. A few years before on Everest, a French expedition had killed six yaks and shortly afterwards six climbers had perished in an avalanche; three yaks were slaughtered by a Japanese expedition to Dhaulagiri and a few days before our own disaster, three of their party had fallen to their deaths. For each slaughtered yak, one dead Sahib!

"Christ!" said the Old Man, hands deep in his pockets, firmly rooted on his bandy legs. "We only just missed that!"

"Thank God it was no worse in that case", said Piussi.

"If we'd had the big avalanche in the night, none of us would have stood a chance in the cold and dark."

"It doesn't bear thinking about. Middle of the night, no torch, running about half-naked at minus fifteen degrees."

This remark of Piussi's had the effect of raising the spirits of the group. Some of them laughed at the thought of five figures crawling about in the snow in their underpants. The Old Man got a bit irritated. He had surmounted many difficult situations in his time; he wasn't to be easily defeated.

"We won't let ourselves be driven away by an avalanche!"

This was Ignazio Piussi again. With his embroidered Tibetan hat and his drooping moustache, he looked like a Mongolian prince. This 40-year old from Friuli still had the look of a cheeky boy. In temperament he was more Austrian than Italian, more poacher than mountaineer. He was respected by all the group and could have easily led the expedition. He was, however, an experienced wood-cutter and preferred to build a cable railway between Camp I and an intermediate camp at 6,400 metres. This magnificent rope lift in the middle of the Lhotse Face was now finished and ready for use, the crowning achievement of his audacious alpine career (first winter ascent of the Civetta Northwest Face, Central Pillar of Freney on Mont Blanc, first ascent of the North Pillar of the Cima Su Alto on the Civetta). It was a cable railway with suspension and hauling ropes, two wooden supports and a winch at the top station. I had been very sceptical about the project at the start, but with Piussi, anything was possible.

Once, when he was in the Julian Alps where he had begun his career as poacher and mountaineer, he had carried two chamois up a 400 metre rockface to avoid being caught by the game-keeper. The keeper, poor man, had bivouaced at the foot of this 'impossible' wall, con-

41

Ignazio Piussi, climber and poacher, constructed a rope railway up part of the South Face of Lhotse to ensure quicker and easier transport of food and equipment.

vinced he would soon catch Piussi, but Ignazio was already over the mountain and away. Climbing and hunting for Piussi were one and the same thing. He thus became a climber with a very well-developed instinctive sense. The game-keeper soon realised that he would never catch Ignazio on the job, so instead of camping out under the cliffs any more, he waited for him outside his door. One day he got such a beating that since then Piussi has never more been worried by game-keepers. Unfortunately, he was not so lucky before the justices.

The very fact that Piussi was keen to continue with the expedition, infused fresh courage into most of the others. The basic facts hadn't changed. Avalanches can happen on such undertakings, and a climber must accept that.

"Who is going to shit his pants just because of two dust clouds?"

"We'll move Base Camp and carry on."

Gigi Alippi was also keen to continue. He was well respected for his quiet thoughtfulness and his decision helped to unite the party.

"We'll have to be careful with our Expedition Reports. If the Press get onto the fact that we had our Base Camp swept away, the next you know, we'll all be reported dead."

"That's right", Gogna nodded.

In the end we were all agreed that Base Camp should be moved further down the valley into the sloping basin on the right-hand opposite Island Peak. We would be protected there from powder avalanches by a ridge. And we would send a cautious progress report to Italy with the postscript "All safe."

Now we just wanted to get on with it.

Only the youngest among us still wanted to go home, preferably today rather than tomorrow. Fausto Lorenzi, a Junior Officer in an Army Mountain School in Aosta, and Mario Conti both asked Cassin if they could go down into the valley at least. They wanted to recover from the shock before venturing on the face again.

When it came to setting up a new abode, each of us had his own particular rituals. The Old Man simply levelled a patch of ground, laid out his tent on it, and put it up, pronto! Just like that. Sandro spent so many hours getting himself together that in the end he had to make do with any place that was left. Curnis, after he had got his tent up, spent days at a stretch prodding about in the avalanche snow, as if he would keep himself busy during the last weeks of the expedition, just doing this. Piussi, who was going to share the big frame tent with Guggiati, our honorary doctor, set about with great flourish to collect an assortment of stone debris, then he dug a large hole and built sturdy walls on the valley side. It seemed for all the world as if he intended to erect a whole house.

As for me – burned child that I was – I found a safe spot under a rock overhang about 100 metres away from the rest of the camp and put up my 2-man tent there. I would be even safer than others in this spot, unless half of the Lhotse Face chose to break off and then my eyrie too would vanish with the rest.

The others refused to believe that it was for safety reasons I isolated myself under the overhang. They knew that in a few weeks my wife would be joining me, and smiled knowingly.

"A fine little love nest you have here!" said one.

"Do you want a hand decorating it?" asked another.

I just laughed.

43

A NEW START
AND OLD PROBLEMS

It was light when, awakened by voices, I opened my eyes. Compared to the old 3-man tent, my new tent seemed narrow. I was still lying in my sleeping bag and could feel the warmth of the sun through the tent roof. Half an hour later we all sat around the breakfast table. The atmosphere felt strange in our new mess tent.

"Where are Conti and Lorenzi", someone asked.

"And Leviti – he's missing too", it suddenly struck us.

"Perhaps they couldn't stand it without any girls any longer, suggested Piussi.

"The shock of the avalanche has unnerved them."

"What the hell do you mean?" Piussi sprang to their defence, "They only need to unwind, that's all. They're only young."

"Not so young – they had their eyes open on the way in all right. I saw Lorenzi ogling all the village beauties. He may be young, but he's old enough for that! What's the betting he's gone down to Namche Bazar to try his luck."

"You're probably right. They'll be back when they've had their fling."

"Good shock therapy"

"We could all do with some of that!"

"You could always try your hand with one of the Sherpa girls who bring up the wood and potatoes each week." This remark was directed at Piussi.

"You must be joking! They couldn't bring up enough wood to heat all the water they would need for a good wash!"

Since the avalanche there was much more of this kind of talk than before. It might seem like schoolboy humour, but there was more to it than that. The great vacuum that followed the avalanche brought with it a heightened awareness of life and an urge to enjoy it to the full. The elemental craving for a woman, a wife, follows a near escape so strongly that it is as if lust alone could banish fear.

"We can't all wangle it like Reinhold. Lucky sod's got his wife coming up to Base Camp."

I joked, "She brings me luck. I've always reached the summit when she's around."

"Then we should have had her here from the beginning."

"Imagine what it would be like if everyone brought his wife or girlfriend", pondered Curnis.

"Bloody murder!"

"I wouldn't say that. I've always thought it would be nice to have a mixed expedition where the women took care of all the cooking and looked after Camp I."

Some of us laughed.

"They would never get up as far as Camp I."

"That's where you're wrong. Women are tougher than you think at altitude. I learned that on Noshaq. The higher we went, the better they performed. With the men it's usually the other way round."

"They've got more staying power than men, too", said Sandro, agreeing with me.

"Anghileri got out at the right time. He'll be home by now. His worries are all over."

Curnis had touched on a sore spot. Feelings were mixed over Anghileri's departure.

Mario Curnis, from Bergamo, was not such a brilliant climber as Anghileri, but he was a better mountaineer, perhaps the most competent all-rounder among us. He had been on several expeditions – twice to the Andes and to Everest – he was safe and fast, particularly on mixed terrain. He didn't say much but when he did open his mouth, everyone listened.

"Anghileri once said there weren't just fifteen of us here, but a hundred. Our mothers, wives and children were all here too. This kind of experience is important to a man. The farther away I am from my wife, the closer she seems to me, the more I feel I understand her."

There was a long silence.

"If Anghileri felt his wife was that close, why did he get so homesick?"

Everyone was listening intently to Giuseppe Alippi.

"Yes, why?" replied Gigi (Det's namesake) and continued with conviction, "Anghileri should have stayed. I was on McKinley once when I was twenty-three. For ten days Jack Canali and I were alone on the glacier, miles from anyone. I was desperate, so desperate I cried. But I didn't let him see I was crying."

"An expedition demands sacrifices over a long period. It shows people in their true light, shows what they are capable of."

All in all, the team didn't completely condemn Anghileri's defection. After seven weeks we had become sworn friends even though we

45

hardly knew each other beforehand. We might argue about Anghileri amongst ourselves, but we would defend him to the hilt against anyone else. Whatever had happened, he was still one of us.

After my fourth mug of tea, I noticed that the mist outside was getting thicker. The wind began to blow in gusts and it got very cold. Then towards mid-day the wind almost died away and in its place we heard the rhythmic pattering of hailstones on the tarpaulin roof.

For a change, I decided to tidy out my tent. The weather had been bad for a week and everything was soaked through. We had been up to Camp II again in the meantime, but were driven back by new snow and avalanche danger. Also I had been smitten with some tummy-bug or other and felt quite wretched. The sun came out for an hour during the morning, so I spread out my mildewed bits and pieces on the tent roof and with the bag for my down jacket, swept the groundsheet, throwing out pebbles, dust and grass onto the little terrace outside the door. Everything smelt of mould and sweat. It was a wonder that we too hadn't slowly begun to moulder.

The face reared vertically above us, a thin curtain of mist draped from its ramparts. As the mists shifted and parted, different portions of the wall became momentarily visible and when, through a hole in the clouds, one suddenly glimpsed the summit, 3,500 metres above, it was like something from another world.

The spirits of the team had sunk to an all-time low. The old good-humoured bantering had long ceased. Piussi survived this dismal interlude the best. He turned his tent into a kind of bar, open to one and all, and each night after our evening meal, we would all congregate in Piussi's 'Night Club'. There we argued, drank and played cards. When we were visited by a wandering Italian, who had run away from his wife and spent two years in Australia, the tent also throbbed with music. We had finally found someone who could play the guitar and soon we were all singing. Morale lifted.

Some of us had been affected more than others by this process of mental deterioration. It showed itself in different ways; grumbling at the Sherpas in the kitchen, finding fault with this or that equipment. It was even worse if you were sick and just had to lie alone in your narrow tent for days on end. Eventually you developed an obsessive dread of going out at all.

The songs we sang in the evenings, often to words of our own composition, grew daily more full of obscenities, more irreverent to both Church and State. Nothing escaped our satire. We lyricised about the Holy Joseph as a homosexual, pussies (both hairy and cleanshaven), the Pope and the Lord Bishops with their armament works and pill factories. Holy land of Italy! Our conversations too mirrored the

Italy of the Twentieth Century. Our expedition was like a tiny Italian State transported into the Himalayas. A handful of sensitive but disorderly people with a system of elaborate rules which were mostly disregarded, fond of wine and beer, quick to passion, and as quickly deflated. In spite of this – or perhaps because of it – from a human angle, this expedition ranks as my happiest Himalayan experience. I have been away with Germans and Austrians but never before felt this immediacy and intimacy with a team. National expeditions tend to reflect the characteristics of the country from which they spring, of this I am sure. Thus an Austrian Expedition will be run on the lines of a small Austrian State, a German one on German lines, British on British lines, and so on. Our Lhotse expedition had no conventional rules and regulations; we always had the opportunity to voice our own opinions and would take all decisions democratically. Cassin was no authoritarian leader, he was more like a father to us. Often he sat in our Night Club till the small hours, laughing and exchanging stories. He was one of us.

Piussi was not completely in agreement with this large expedition concept. "For this kind of face", he would say, "speed is the essence, and you can only get that with a more flexible expedition. The classical system of months of preparation, high camps and an army of porters – that's a thing of the past!"

"This kind of climb is so demanding, one way or another, I don't believe anyone could climb it as a single rope party. It's true Bonatti has pleaded for a more sporting approach to difficult climbing on high mountains, but not this one – that's going too far!" Arcari's answer was delivered with quiet deliberation. He was a friend of Walter Bonatti, coming from the same town of Monza, and was one of the most experienced members of the expedition. He had been on four expeditions and done nearly all the great routes of the Alps.

"If you ask me", said Gogna "Expeditions like this are quite absurd." He wanted to end this conversation.

"Why did you agree to come then?"

"After Annapurna – I wanted another go at a big mountain." Piussi, who had just been outside, came back into the tent. The frozen ground seemed to shudder under his heavy tread. Not that Ignazio was fat but he was extraordinarily big and powerful. He stood a head taller than any of the rest of us. He could crush a mug into a pellet of tin with his bare fingers.

"I don't say it will happen right away. But sometime in the future an eight-thousander will be climbed alpine-style by a party of two. It will need real men to do it, not pant-wetters who cry 'Mama mia' as soon as the wind gets up."

Piussi had brought the conversation full-circle. He was in fact quite pleased with the results of this expedition. He had learned to take triumph and defeat as they came.

"What we want is smaller mountains, fewer people and no fixed ropes!" This was Barbacetto's simple recipe.

"How I hate all this jumaring! Climbing fixed ropes is the worst kind of masturbation. A thousand metres at a time, sometimes two or three days on a fucking fixed rope. Clip on and shove, shove, shove. It makes me puke." Now that Gogna had so eloquently expressed his disgust for our classical expedition methods, he seemed to brighten.

"These jumar clamps weren't invented in the Himalayas, you know." laughed Piussi, and treated us to the tale of his winter epic on the Northwest Face of the Civetta.

There was still snow on the ground as the Italian Lhotse South Face expedition marched towards Base Camp in March 1975. Porters and a yak on the way from Dingboche to the Nuptse Glacier. In the background, the summit of Ama Dablam, the holy mountain.

Climbing on the Lhotse South Face. Below Camp I, 6000 m.

△
View from the
Lhotse South Face to
the east towards
Makalu (8475 m),
scene of my failure
in 1974.

◁ After the second
avalanche on Lhotse
Base Camp (5300m)
destroyed tents and
injured Sherpas;
compressed snow
and a general feeling
of shock.

A 30m ice bulge at 7000m blocked the route on the Lhotse South Face.

VERTICAL WORLD
ABOVE THE CLOUDS

The daily Serkim prayer was over. For half an hour the Sherpa lama had sat in lotus position on a rock above the kitchen and led the singing from a book. The voices of the other Sherpas joined in with a kind of choral humming, above which one could now and again make out the mysterious words "Hargallio", (we are going to God).

Even the cook under his canopy, rattling his pots and pans, seemed to be taking more notice of the monotonous chanting than the breakfast he was preparing for the Sahibs. And Angtsering, whose job it was to distribute the Sherpa loads, was giving them out in time to the undulating rhythm of the worshippers.

Finally the lama was silent. He was a large young man, a half-brother of Angtsering. He placed a wooden cover over the open leaves of his book and climbed down from his altar-stone. The aromatic smell of the incense lingered in the branches and spread its pleasant fragrance around.

The camp resumed its habitual disorder. The cook's boy brought the breakfast into the mess tent, and the Sherpas crouched down near their packed rucksacks and shovelled rice noodles into their mouths with their fingers. What vast quantities of rice they are able to consume so early in the morning!

For our final attempt we were going to put in all the high altitude porters. With Cassin, I had worked out an exact plan of who should be in each high camp during the next few days. Mario Curnis and I were to reconnoitre the summit wall and we therefore set off first. The Sherpas, who were to accompany us, gave us each a handful of sacred rice, which we were to strew at the foot of all dangerous pitches as they always took care to do. The fleecy clouds which glided slowly across the sky endowed the day with a kind of youthful promise. The pessimism which had enveloped me during the last few days was dispelled in the face of such spring-like freshness and I was soon moving briskly, full of renewed hope.

What was it Piussi said before he went to bed?

"If you stop talking about victory but simply believe in it, then it will come."

I turned my gaze to the summit buttress, where a gust of wind had just whipped up a plume of snow, and I climbed upwards past the old Base Camp site. Much of the avalanched snow had now melted away and I could see crushed tents, bent aluminium poles and heaps of rubble where our store huts had been. We were still missing some vital items of our equipment.

"'Insatiable is my thirst for danger'", quoted Curnis next to me, laughing.

"Who said that – Lammer?"

"'I am ready to cast my life aside like a broken alpenstock'", he continued.

But the image didn't fit Mario at all, I knew. There were none of us ready to do that. We were prepared for fear and failure, in our attempt to reach our objective, but drew the line at suicide. But were we not already too late? We had not yet placed our third high camp and it was now the beginning of May. Had we perhaps not lost the gamble for the Lhotse Face already, with the passing of April? We didn't seem to have come to terms with it at all. With the Lhotse Face, I mean, but I could just as well have said, with the full force of the Himalayas themselves, the eight-thousanders, this environment so alien and hostile. It was this force which directed our thinking and shaped us perhaps more than our mountaineering ethics and literature. This landscape that boasts not a flat, easy spot anywhere, is so overpowering. Within a few kilometres, the country embraces the pitiless hell of the 'Death Zone' and the peaceful harmony of the lama monasteries. The climate with its extremes of cold and heat, reminds one of a smith compounding fire and water to harden his steel. By day the sun, vertically above, makes of it a desert; by night, the snow and storms, a polar waste.

If an average citizen were to expend the energy in three months that a climber needs to ascend an eight-thousander, he would age ten years overnight. The constant storms, wild and violent, can fill the most balanced of men with inner turmoil, reduce them to a state of despair like shipwrecked mariners.

The terrain is so steep, the climate so harsh, danger so unremitting, that there is no escape from them, and the summits far above seem so remote, one cannot believe they may be trodden by mortals like ourselves. All this we knew clearly enough, and had to rely rather less on physical but on logical considerations.

Mario and I climbed up through scoured gullies, around ice pinnacles shaped like giant mushrooms, inched our way along foot-wide ledges, always attached to the fixed rope. Camp I was in a terrible state, everything jumbled about as never before, and all soaking wet. The two sleeping mats had vanished, there were no matches and the pans were filthy. At 3 the next morning it was bright and clear, the Milky Way a bold white strip across the dark sky, Orion poised over Ama Dablam. By 5 o'clock a few stars still twinkled through thin mist, and the first glimmers of dawn lit the sky. Two hours later we were away. The rock ridge above rose like a mighty sugar tower; it was coated with ice and its holds all sloped downwards. It was hard to distinguish the various curves of the ridge as cloud infilled all the hollows. Our eyes smarting, we picked our way up to Camp II. A flat blanket of mist lay below us, ashen and unreal. Had the Monsoon come already?

The silence was absolute. Over the clouds, only the summit of Makalu could be seen. It floated like an island in the East, its flanks shimmering with ice. There was nothing else in our semi-circle of vision. With the ground invisible below, we felt peculiarly remote from reality.

It had taken us five hours to break through the cloud barrier, five hours in knee-deep snow, probing and climbing to reach Camp II. We were quite exhausted and threw ourselves down to rest. We could not sleep but simply sat there for a few hours; then, pulling myself together, I brewed some tea. The crescent sky viewed through the entrance of the box tent was striped with bright light as the sun began to sink behind Nuptse.

Since the avalanche catastrophe we hadn't killed any more yaks, and the two Alippis had dismantled their bird traps. They had constructed a sort of guillotine from sticks and flakes of stone, in the hopes of catching a few Snow-Cocks which were to be seen from time to time around Base Camp. Naturally they would have preferred a Golden Eagle, but they only saw one.

It wasn't that we believed the superstition – one dead yak, one dead climber – but we were taking care not to offend the Gods any more. We had made that promise to our Sherpas and intended to respect the native customs. It was forbidden to kill any animal above Dingpoche. Simply by being there and having the intention to climb so high a mountain, we had intruded into the lives of the Nepalese. We climbers – by which I mean all the climbers that have ever come here – have caused the inhabitants to wonder at our technology, but we have at the same time endangered their own cultural identity. Our ways of camping, cooking, doctoring are for us the only ways of doing these things, but – like it or not – they have shattered the religious and moral structure of life in these mountain villages. Every fresh expedition destroys a little bit more of the indigenous culture. With our radio equipment, for example, we arbitrarily cross the natural boundaries of place and time. With our oxygen apparatus, we intrude upon the abodes of the Gods. We are, therefore, in the eyes of these people, capable of performing miracles, such as they would normally only attribute to people specially selected by the Gods. And if we can work such miracles, then they feel we must be in some way superior to them, both intellectually and from a religious point of view.

Before each crevasse and awkward pitch, the Sherpas who had come up with Mario and I, scattered their holy rice and murmured their sibilant prayers. And we in our turn were especially careful crossing drifts and crevasses, traversing slopes of new snow. Against avalanches, storms and gravity we had no power. The Gods remain superior after all.

The cloud-front to the south was steel blue. From the summit of Ama Dablam hung a banner of cloud like a huge Tibetan prayer flag. One could now see down to Base Camp. The ground was back with us.

I woke up the next morning to the certainty that I had failed my Abitur, my school-leaving certificate. Memories of those examinations and of my professors flashed back to me, along with anxiety at the prospect of facing life without the certificate. The image of my last year at college swept over me like the mist from the valley. Though this was ten years ago, it was as clear as yesterday, and I could see clearly the sarcastic grin of my engineering tutor, Professor Wackernell. Like toys from a box, I picked up the pieces of my dream and built them up like bricks. My winter attempt on the Matterhorn North Face, the Bonatti Route, I had done in school time; it had taken a week. I wrote out and signed my own letter of excuse as I was already twenty-one. Professor Zani, our German master had me on the carpet for that. Result – no Abitur!

Nevertheless, I had been a good scholar and eventually passed the Abitur with high marks. I tried again to get my memories into order, but it was like going around in a circle in the dark, failing to find the only exit. It was not the first time this dream had troubled me. I had had it before several times, always on expeditions and mostly at altitude. It always concentrated on that first failure, taking no account of the later success. Like soap bubbles the images of my last months at school floated before me and burst before I had a chance to catch hold of them.

"You are surely not going to let yourself be influenced by Professor Zani" – had I really had the cheek to say that to Engineer Wackernell? I hadn't meant it seriously, but it had failed me.

A year later I had sat the Abitur again privately and passed. My father had refused to give me any more money and so I had had to work to earn it. I was proud of the result.

How many hours had I been awake – or half awake? It must be nearly 4 o'clock by now as the morning rays were shining on the yellow perlon roof of the box-tent. With the back of my hand I wiped the condensation from my eyes; it ran down my cheeks and stung my peeling sunburn.

"The plaster's coming off!" murmured Mario from his sleeping bag as he watched me pull the bits of dead skin from my nose.

"Hardly surprising with that sun shining through the haze yesterday. No face cream would be much good against that."

A day later we climbed with Det Alippi and two Sherpas to establish Camp III. We had already pioneered and fixed ropes on much of the route; we wanted to place the tent under the 500 metre vertical summit wall. Det was leading; like a machine he ploughed forwards. He would pull one leg out of the snow until his knee-joint formed an acute angle, then plunge it down again and repeat the process with the other leg. Each time he sank up to his knees in the loose powder snow. It was bloody murder.

At 41, Det was, after Cassin, the second oldest member of the team, but when it came to stamina and willpower, he left the rest of us in the shade. The palms of his hands were like baked clay and the skin of his face, like leather. Slim and small, he was particularly well adapted for climbing at great height. He was not one of the 'stars' of the team, he had no sensational first ascents to his credit and was somewhat disillusioned by the 'prima donnas' of the party. He demonstrated – half consciously, half unconsciously – that up here it was not the climber's name that counted, but the man himself.

Det was feeling his old self again now. During the last few weeks he had waited in vain for news from his wife and was often very upset. Whenever the post-runner came up and brought nothing for him, the others used to rib him:

"You should have left her enough money for writing paper and stamps." This from one of his Lecco friends who liked to make out that Det was a skinflint.

"He really thinks she will wait for him", taunted another.

"Three months in the Himalaya, and his wife all alone at home."

"So what about that?" said Det.

"No woman will stand for that!"

This bantering went on week after week, every time the runner came up. The longer Det was without a letter, the worse it got.

"She hasn't the time to write to you."

"Why not?"

"Because she's found herself someone else, you credulous fool!"

57

"Who could she find?"

"The milkman – or the postman, perhaps."

This always made Det furious and he would stalk off to his tent to write a bitter letter to his wife, always closing with the query "Have you perhaps found yourself another Det?"

Of course there was no other Det, but how he went on about it! For hours on end. The poor man was in torment.

All I wanted to do was to stand there and let my racing heart quieten down, my over-worked lungs pump more slowly. My glance swept over the endless snow slopes; the seracs and glaciers were barely visible in the light mist. The wind on the nearby summit ridge no longer howled, it whispered. A flurry of sleet caught me in the face. Like whiplashes it burnt into my raw skin.

The altimeter showed 7,100 metres. It was another 100 metres yet to the end of the ice ramp, if the map at Base Camp on which we had counted off the contours, was correct.

Now I climbed first, taking extreme care where I set my feet. In this half light the surface of the snow was indeterminable. I noticed that I was automatically testing the ground before venturing each new step. A feeling of hopelessness gripped me. Nowhere was there a safe place to camp and the face appeared to be getting steeper. The wide ramp had disappeared and we were climbing in a vast vertical ice-wilderness. It seemed to me that we had been climbing for days, one behind the other. Not another living soul on this forsaken piece of Earth. Were we still on Lhotse?

It was then I saw horizontally above me, a dark band and pulling myself up on my axe, found myself staring over the edge of a crevasse, a marginal crevasse. The lower lip was sound enough and despite the mist, I could see that the upper lip projected like the eaves of a roof. How was it to the right? A dozen steps brought me teetering to the edge of a sheer drop. The crevasse fell away to my left, and to my right was the mountain face. And the distance between the upper and lower lips had widened. Too dangerous, I turned round and came back to my original position. Mario stood next to me, "Will it do?" he asked.

"Yes, if we dig the box-tent right in."

"Yes, we'll push it right inside, then we'll be safe as houses."

The Sherpas had taken off their loads and were starting back down to Camp II, with Det leading them. Mario and I sorted out the gear – one tent; two sleeping mats, barely more than a centimetre thick; one stove; food for two days, and a shovel. Climbing and personal equipment were still in our rucksacks.

Meanwhile the mist had sunk lower. The bright blanket of cloud had settled below us, still and smooth as a millpond. The horizon might have been drawn with a compass, it described such a perfect arc. No peaks rose above the dazzling cloud. How small our field of vision had become.

It took two hours before our tent was up, its rear half well back inside the mountain, the front projecting slightly but protected by the upper lip of the crevasse. An avalanche might catch us, but it wouldn't carry us away. But despite this, we were a little afraid. We were so tired we could hardly eat and it took tremendous effort to put on our frozen outer boots. It wasn't until we had left the tent and were roped up that I managed to recover my peace of mind. Defiantly we braved the rising storm.

After two hours we had fixed 100 metres of rope above us on the face. That was all we had up here. In the afternoon two Sherpas brought up another rope – our next day's work.

Night came, but there was no question of sleep. We each knew the other was awake, unable to relax, not daring to breathe in order to hear what might be happening outside. It was all quiet. We listened. Nothing. Suddenly, first a rumble, then a roar – Whoom – boom – boom – boom. . . . We jumped up, appalled. A snow slide was sweeping over our tent. Would it take us with it? We were petrified. Then suddenly all was quiet again. The flat roof sagged badly in the middle, and hoar frost lay finger-thick on the walls. We had been lucky, once again. In a quarter of an hour we were both asleep.

When I woke the next morning I attempted to compare this expedition with my former mountaineering experiences. First of all there had been easy tours like the Sass Rigais, my first three-thousander, when I was five years old. Sunny alpine meadows and warm Dolomite rock. Later I climbed some of the hardest walls in the Alps, some menacing gullies, and progressed to some of the steepest faces on the highest mountains of the world: the Rupal Flank on Nanga Parbat, the South Face of Manaslu, Makalu South Face, and now the South Face of Lhotse. Each steeper and more difficult than the last, culminating in this vertical wall above us, this 500 metre thrust into the Death Zone, with which we would have to come to grips during the next ten hours. Vertical rock upon rock, a perpendicular desert, as desolate as despair.

How gladly I would have exchanged the prospect now, what I wouldn't give to have Uschi instead of this cursed wall! What a fool I had been! Was the challenge of the Lhotse South Face more important than my love for her? Perhaps I had been too arrogant, too ambitious to give anything up, to sacrifice my place on this expedition. And where was love without sacrifice?

Before I left Camp II – more than 40 hours ago – I had written to

59

Uschi and stuck her last letter to me in my rucksack. She had been to Munich, felt lonely, otherwise all went well with her. She had been working in the garden in Villnöss, and had even planted some tomatoes. I like tomatoes, but I hardly thought they would ripen at that altitude, 1,400 metres.

Since then, I had climbed for hours through snow and steep ice. Only now up in Camp III as I re-read her letter, things became clear to me. I was forced to confess, as I had done many times before, that I was an egoist. Long letters home describing this or that progress or failure, couldn't gainsay the fact. On my earlier expeditions, I had written less frequently and then almost exclusively about the mountain; in those days winning or losing were still the most important things to me. My letters home to Uschi these days had become somewhat monotonous – I don't mean boring, exactly, but too rational. I expected her to understand from them all the things I couldn't express. More than that, I expected her to be in agreement with me. I hadn't got it quite straight yet, but as I saw it at this moment, my egoism was something that couldn't be changed. There were reasons for that. My reasons. But everything kept coming back to the single fact that I was an egoist. There was no question of giving up now – I did not even want to think about it; reaching the summit was still a possibility, I still had a chance to make it.

Mario prussiked up to me from the spot we had reached the day before. Belayed to two pegs, he slowly forced the rope through the brake. One centimetre – rest – another centimetre. The rock was rotten, very rotten indeed. When I twisted my head round to see what it was like ahead, I had the impression that the whole mountain was about to crumble away.

"Watch out! Below!"

I continually had to warn Mario of falling stones, they would suddenly appear in the air, tiny black dots overhead, then whirr past and hit the ice below like shrapnel.

We reached the crack which split the second half of the summit wall right across, obliquely from left to right. We were at a height of 7,500 metres. With my axe hanging from my wrist and my gloves dangling on strings, I forced my way over smooth, virgin slabs, straddled a high chimney and reached a vertical crack. My crampons grated against the rock. The peg which I tried to insert in a long crack would not go in. Five more blows with my hammer and it held. I threaded a double rope through it, snapped in a karabiner and there was my intermediate belay. I wanted to attempt the crack at a run. Either I made it in a single thrust, or I felt I would not make it at all. My strength and determination were not up to prolonged effort.

I got as far as the middle. As I straightened up in the last two footholds, I couldn't see any more holds above me and the rock was very steep. Damn!

"Watch out!"

Mario looked up, his hat covered in snow. I couldn't move to give him a sign because I would surely have lost my balance. Then I saw a knob of rock as big as a man's fist; with three stout blows from my axe, the ice splintered off it. Quickly I fumbled for a sling from my harness, put it around the knob, tested it to see if it would hold, then, thus belayed, I swung across to a ledge on my right. Saved.

I was ready to bring up Mario, who was belayed to a wedge and two diagonal pitons.

"Come on!"

He had just banged out the first peg, leaving the second for the fixed rope, when a stone avalanche hit us. For a full five minutes, the crashing and whistling of stones was all about us. Mario and I stood pressed into the wall, our rucksacks on our heads, and waited. At first we were rigid with fear, then submitted to our fate. If we could only have crawled inside the mountain.

This was too much. A stench of sulphur hung about and the air seemed to be still vibrating as we roped back down. Down to the tent, and on down to Base. We had had more than enough for the time being.

A BRUSH WITH DEATH

"Camp III to Base Camp, Camp III to Base Camp!"

Four of us sat round Cassin in the mess tent drinking midday tea. From the 3,000 cans of beer we had brought with us, only one full crate remained and we wanted to save that. It was windy and cold. I shivered despite my hat and duvet jacket.

Cassin picked up the receiver.

"Base Camp to Camp III, I can hear you."

"Leviti here. Sandro has just gone down to Camp II. Tomorrow Sereno and I will take over from where the other two left off today. Around 7,500 metres, to the left of the Messner route, it looks as if it will go, as Reinhold suggested. It's a bit broken, but there's not so much danger from stonefalls as there was the other way."

"Understood. That is good news."

"I don't much care for the campsite up here; I think I'll move the tent."

"Where do you want to move it to?"

"Farther out. The upper lip of the crevasse could easily break off."

I gave Cassin a nudge. No, they mustn't do that. If the box tent was only a single metre further out, it could get carried away by an avalanche. And I quickly made a rough sketch of the position at Camp III and pushed it under his nose, so that he could see for himself. I begged him again to forbid their moving the tent. Dig it further in, if you like, but not out. That would be too dangerous.

The Old Man did as I said. What we could not know at the time was that we had averted a major catastrophe by this decision.

It occurred a few minutes before the 7 o'clock radio call. An avalanche rolled over Camp III whilst Aldo Leviti and Sereno Barbacetto were inside. They cowered inside the pitch dark box, pressed against the innermost corner. Their clothes were wet and covered in a layer of ice. Barbacetto could feel something as hard as concrete digging into him. It was the cooking stove and he could feel the shape of it so plainly it was almost as if he could see it in the dark.

There were a few stunned moments before the two crouching men realised exactly what had happened and then, instinctively, they

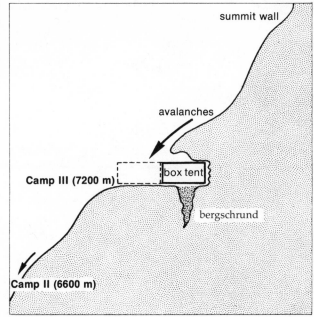

Camp III on the Lhotse South Face.
– – – – Position in which Leviti wished to place the box tent.

began to sort things out. The avalanche had swept over the tent and into the crevasse, at the same time packing all the spaces between the walls of the tent and the mountain with granular new snow which it had peeled from the summit crags. Luckily, there was just enough air left in the tent to enable them to breathe. Despite their terror when the tent caved in on them, they made no desperate struggle, but paused to consider the situation. And it was doubtless due to this presence of mind that they later emerged alive from the demolished tent. Instinctively Aldo seized his sunglasses, broke the glass and made a slit in the bulging wall of the tent. It immediately gaped open like a wound.

Aldo's voice, as he reported the situation over the radio, betrayed the ordeal they had just been through.

"We've been caught in an avalanche. It looks grim!"

The Old Man began to tremble all over. There were tears in his eyes and he kept asking the question that was uppermost in all our minds – could they hold out? What could we do from Base Camp to help them, he wanted to know. As it was night there was nothing we could do for the time being. Leviti and Barbacetto were stuck in the crevasse, 2,000 metres above us. The wind was blowing in, swirling powder snow all around inside the tent. The pair of them were near to total collapse.

The Old Man didn't sleep a wink all night. In his anxiety for the two

63

The great Riccardo Cassin, first to climb the Walker Spur on the Grandes Jorasses, the South Face of Mount McKinley, the Badile Wall and the North Face of the Cima Ovest. He was the father figure of the Lhotse Expedition.

men, he stayed till well after midnight in the mess tent with his radio. Later he lay awake in his sleeping bag, the radio switched on beside him. Once again his paternal instincts took possession of him. During the whole expedition he had always been closely involved with each one of us, taking a personal interest in our problems, ready with advice and comfort, and tactfully smoothing out any arguments that blew up amongst us.

Riccardo Cassin, without doubt the outstanding climber of the inter-war years, worked like a Berserker. His large, expressive hands still possessed incredible strength and I recalled how in 1935 he had pitonned his way across the North Face of the Cima Ovest; with his apelike arms, he had hauled himself up the first ascent of the Torre Trieste on the Civetta; also made the first ascents of the South Face of the Cima Piccolissima, North East Face of the Badile, Walker Spur, North Face of the Aiguille Leschaux, Terza Sorella Northwest Face, etc. Cassin remained active after the war too, and it was these exploits that marked him above his contemporaries. In 1958 he led the Italian Gasherbrum IV Expedition, in 1961 he climbed the South Face of Mount McKinley and in 1969 was with a Lecco team on Jirishanca. Lhotse was to be the fulfilment of his greatest ambition, a direttissima on what was probably the most difficult Big Wall in the World.

And now, here he was, all washed up. The problems had now

grown too much for him. He was *too* good and *too* paternal for a modern expedition leader. We could all see by looking at him that our hopes had crumbled to dust.

What lent Cassin such status? It wasn't just his age. It was partly his achievements but, though his style of climbing was attractive it was not grounds enough to inspire such veneration. Rebuffat captured it when he said Cassin was a gentleman, modest yet assured, prudent yet experienced. Each of us were proud to be with him. He could laugh so warm-heartedly and was always ready to flirt and chat up the girls. His face was constantly mobile but always the same – honest and open; it radiated both purpose and calm.

Cassin's face creased into a relieved smile as he went forward to meet the two survivors, just down from Camp III. He embraced them fondly. They had been spared; they lived! In the afternoon, Aldo Leviti, one of the youngest of the team and a participant of the Italian 1973 Everest Expedition, gave us his report of what happened. Bent over the table in the mess tent, resting on his elbows and nervously clutching and unclutching his hands, his eyes still inflamed, he told his story.

"By around midnight we had got the tent clear enough to be able to squat in the far corner. The storm didn't let up all night. Shortly after the first avalanche, a second one rattled down close by. Then another, slightly to the right of us before we had finished digging ourselves out from the first one. It roared down like a cataract over the top lip of our crevasse and heaped up in front of us; luckily it didn't quite block our entrance or we might well have suffocated. It's hard to be exact but it went on for about two hours, then it stopped and began to snow. By then it was morning, somewhere between 3 and 5 o'clock. We stayed inside our hole, rubbing each other to keep warm. As soon as it was light, we crawled out. We were covered in snow from head to foot, there was ice all in our hair. Not at all pleasant. Below us the whole slope was made up of avalanche debris. It was still quite cloudy with gusts of wind and spindrift blowing off the ridge. Not too bad for coming down if all the fixed ropes were still in place."

"What about the stove? Did you have it on when the first avalanche struck?"

"Oh yes, I was cooking at the time. Sereno suddenly pulled me back and at the same moment the front of the tent collapsed like an empty paper bag. The flame went out of course, but the gas was still on."

We all sat for hours mulling over the situation. All enthusiasm for continuing the climb had ebbed away. We had just learned of two other disasters, both on Nuptse, a few kilometres away. The first had wiped out the summit pair; they had simply disappeared. The second

65

hit a party coming down from Camp VII to Camp VI. Their two friends waited in vain for them to appear. Later they found their bodies on the glacier below.

At the same time Radio Nepal reported the success of the Austro-German Expedition to Kangchenjunga. Three parties reached the summit. We were impressed. The news revived our flagging interest somewhat, but we still had reservations.

"It's too dangerous. Just because another expedition has success on an easier route, isn't sufficient cause for us to risk life and limb on this one."

It was nearly the middle of May and we would soon have to pull out in any case. It snowed almost every afternoon already and a bitter southwest wind caught the mighty face square-on with all its force. On the summit ridge it howled like a storm-tossed sea. I sat frequently with the porters in the cookhouse. The pungent smoke and the eddies of wind inflated the orange canopy which, attached to two wooden poles, formed the roof. Drops of condensation plopped into the fire and hissed for a moment before evaporating.

"Japanese ladies' success!" cried Tschottre, our liaison officer. Over the radio he had heard that the Japanese Ladies Everest Expedition had reached the summit. Junko Tabei and a Sherpa were the ones to reach the top. Our Sherpas were jubilant, and not without a measure of malicious glee – a woman on the summit of the world's highest mountain, and we all in Base Camp.

Life at Base Camp was becoming monotonous. The indifference of the demoralised team depressed me. It didn't last long, but long enough to arouse in me the old urge for action. I was determined not to be lulled into inactivity purely on safety grounds and began to work out an alternative objective for the expedition. To have a goal and to believe that it can be reached, is half way to success itself, and at the same time gives a purpose to life. A direct line to the summit was no longer a feasible proposition; the face was too steep and broken, and moreover, completely iced up. I therefore proposed that we should try a different route further to the left, where a ramp and a short spur gave access to the ridge, and it seemed to me that we would arrive at a point on the ridge directly above the Silent Valley (Western Cwm) which ran from the Khumbu Icefall between the North Face of Nuptse and the South-west Face of Everest, to the foot of Lhotse's North Flank. Perhaps from there one could descend the steep snow slopes to the Japanese Ladies, who were still on Everest and would certainly have camps down there. Some us could go westwards, round the base of Nuptse and Lhotse and wait at the foot of Everest for the others to come over the top. We

Junko Tabel the first woman to climb Everest. I met her between expeditions in Katmandu.

all realised that it was now too late to make an attempt on the summit of Lhotse. However, this plan of a traverse of the Nuptse-Lhotse massif was not very well received. When I unfolded it after supper, I could tell from Riccardo's face that since not everyone was in agreement, there would be little chance of successfully carrying out the complicated manoeuvres that would be involved. He had no objections to the plan himself, probably recognising that this last chance should not be rejected out of hand. It might be possible to achieve some success even with only part of the team.

We couldn't just sit here and let ourselves be beaten. The possibility of this traverse seemed to me scarcely less attractive than the Lhotse climb itself. But it took several days before the majority of the team were for my project. Cassin worked out how the high camps should be placed and who should undertake the lead. One team must first fix rope up the last 200 metres to the ridge, then another would attempt the crossing and a second team would follow. This way the first team could reach the ridge relatively easily and then, without having to erect a camp there, could climb down the other side. The second team would follow the first down, but in emergency could bring help from above.

We spent several days discussing all this but in the meantime renewed, unbroken bad weather prevented the plan being seriously attempted.

67

DEFEAT

As I had done after our defeat on Makalu, I now weighed up in my mind the pros and cons of a large expedition. On the one side it offers greater safety, back-up, the possibility of substitution in case of illness, comradeship. On the other hand you must offset the restricted mobility, the long discussions and the team spirit, which, under certain circumstances, can strangle all progress. With careful preparation and the necessary experience, a two-man expedition would not only be quicker and cheaper, but also safer. On any quite large mountain everyone must be completely self-reliant. It is much easier to find a single well-matched partner than ten or fifteen.

Then came the 13th May, the day Cassin formally announced the failure of our expedition. From then on I had but one thought, and longingly I waited for Uschi, who would surely soon be in Base Camp.

Of course at that time I didn't have any idea what had been happening back home in the meantime. A year before I had written to the Pakistani authorities, requesting permission to climb Hidden Peak, but as I hadn't so far received any answer, I no longer expected one and had almost forgotten the whole business. And then: the reply came from Pakistan, the permit* had been granted. Uschi had taken the letter from Rawalpindi to the Mountain Film Festival in Trento, where she had met Peter Habeler and let him into the secret. Peter had already promised to attempt Hidden Peak with me and he was thrilled. But for the time being no-one must know of our hazardous enterprise.

In Trento too, I had won the ITAS prize for my book ''The Seventh Grade'', and as I was away, Uschi had collected the award for me. The President of the Assembly, Senator Spagnolli, pulled her almost half across the table to whisper in her ear, as he handed over the certificate and the prize money – manna from heaven for our lean expedition kitty.

''What did he say'' asked Emanuele Cassara, a journalist, with his pencil eagerly poised.

*To attempt any high peak in Pakistan or Nepal, one needs an Expedition Permit, which has to be applied for at least a year in advance and is difficult to obtain.

"They have reached 7,200 metres and are beginning the traverse to the summit. In a week it will be theirs", answered Uschi.

They both laughed, wishing it might be true, but they had received Italian expedition news before and knew better than to accept it without a pinch of salt.

In ten days at the latest, Uschi would surely be in Base Camp. If she caught a flight the day after the film festival, she would be in Katmandu on 5th May. Two days for obtaining a trekking permit, then the flight to Lukla, two days to Namche Bazar, another to Tengpoche and then two more to get up to Base Camp. In the evenings in my little tent, I remembered all those other times I had been reunited with Uschi after a long separation. In 1971 in late autumn in Karachi, when I was returning from New Guinea; I had bought a new shirt. A few months before in Milan: she had come to the airport in vain because someone had given her the wrong arrival date. A week later she came again and we climbed the Delago-kante on her birthday. She was so surefooted and agile, it was as if she had been climbing all her life. Then, after Manaslu, we met in Munich. That was three years ago. Three years of separations and reunions, sorrow and happiness. At that moment in the airport, there were only two people in the whole world, Uschi and me. I was dizzily happy, over the moon, as she came to me and I held her once more in my arms. Somewhere, far away, were the journalists, friends and well-wishers – somewhere in another world.

Now in the tent, I tried to conjure up her face before me. It was always the same image – her happy, open laugh. Always that and nothing more. How long was her hair when I last saw her? On which cheek was that tiny brown freckle? I couldn't remember. Hard as I tried to picture her face, it remained hazy.

The next morning I asked Cassin if I might go down the valley and meet my wife. He agreed. I wanted to run down all the way till I found her. Piussi would come with me as far as the Japanese Hotel by Khumjung to fetch the money we needed for paying off the porters. Immediately after breakfast we set off. In our rucksacks we carried only our sleeping rolls, a hard loaf and some tins.

After our gruelling experiences in the high snows, this descent was like a return to life. Around Base Camp only tufts of withered grass grew, lower down we came to stunted bushes, then to fresh, green grass and far below in the valley, we could see the occasional strip of woodland and patches of damp earth. Even the sterile upper pastures were occupied. These room-sized, brown-green patches between the rocks were the hill farms, tiny oases at the foot of the eight-thousanders, the impoverished homeland of the Sherpa, the barren grazing of the frugal yak.

When we had come up some six weeks before, I had not really been aware of the subtle change from the last inhabited farmsteads to the moraine debris beneath the glacier. It was all treeless, and it was the prospect of the mountains, with their ever-changing faces, that had fascinated me. Now, as I came down from the high regions, where the rocks were only barely covered with moss and lichen, I was overwhelmed on this spring morning, with all I saw. Patches of snow still lingered on the shady side of the valley and the rhododendron bushes and grass were still crumpled from its weight, but close by, bloomed the first flowers – primulas and tiny bellflowers with bright green, downy leaves.

As we went lower down, the valley filled with cloud. Moisture penetrated our clothes and formed a layer of minute droplets over our pullovers. In less than two hours I had reached the hill above Dingpoche. From the distance, I could just make out the first houses scattered across the valley floor, under the glowering cloud. The tiny fields were ringed by waist-high stone walls, giving them the appearance of empty honeycomb. All around were the stony slopes, grey-brown and apparently untilled. Halfway up the slope on the right hand side of the valley, there was a monastery tucked under a rocky precipice; two windows in a whitewashed wall. Over the lower outskirts of the village, the clouds were constantly moving; new mist was rising and shifting slowly over fields and huts. Houses and walls swam in the all-embracing greyness. It seemed that the mist was trying to conceal the whole village from me. Peering ahead, I quickly passed to the north of the village, then suddenly, between the dappled side of a house and a ruined wall, I saw a yellow fleck. Surely it was a tent – I could not have been mistaken? It must be them! The roof of the tent gleamed through the dark grey-blue mist, and was still visible as fresh waves of fog encircled it.

It was only a dozen more paces to the tent. I could hear voices, but not Uschi's. It was undoubtedly fragments of German. Hesitantly, I drew apart the flaps of the tent. Heidi, Uschi's sister, and Inge, her friend, were there. But where was Uschi? Then I spotted her a little way off, leaning against a wall. I rushed to her side, kissed her, pressing her closely to me and discovering her anew. A light wind ruffled her hair from her brow. It was a moment of supreme joy. My fingers linked with hers, her hair gently brushed my face.

The weather had cleared. Again, a fine mist had been falling all morning, but now the sun broke through the clouds. The fields, the stone slabs on the roofs, the bushes, the drystone walls – all steamed. The water in the narrow irrigation ditches sparkled in the May sunshine. It was four in the afternoon when we set off for a short walk. Hand in hand

70

Uschi Messner at
Dingpoche on her way to
the Lhotse Base Camp.

like children, we wandered across the fields, scrambling over little walls
and sitting for a long time beside a chorten*. We had a glimpse through a
hole in the cloud of the holy mountain, Taboche. Our roving through
the almost deserted village did not cease until dusk. This day had been
the most beautiful of the whole expedition. It was a day in which I not
only met Uschi again, I rediscovered her. And it was a day too, in which
I began to forget all the fine resolutions I had made on Lhotse. For that
evening, Uschi handed over to me the permit for attempting Hidden
Peak in the Karakoram. At first it didn't mean anything to me, or so I
thought, but already subconsciously, I must have been receptive to the
new challenge. It was not long before I had to admit I was ready to take
it on. And it was not until weeks later, after I had set out for Hidden
Peak, that I remembered this day and its decision with sadness.

On the next morning, we sat in Dingpoche on the stone wall of a
potato field, blinking in the sunshine. From the lama's small house,
close by our camp site, rose a thin wisp of smoke that the wind got hold
of and tore into tiny shreds. Uschi told me of her journey; it had been
singularly hectic from the moment she left the Trento festival, all the
way to Katmandu. She was staying with English friends when she got
the news, packed for Nepal at lightning speed, travelled to Munich with
the Britons in a grossly-overloaded car, sat up the whole night talking,

*Symbolic building of lamaistic philosophy; a wayside shrine, mostly found at entrance of
villages, cross-roads, mountain passes.

71

then slept across the seats of a half-empty aeroplane to Delhi.

During the two months of our separation she had not had much time for brooding. Now she was contented and relaxed. She was in top form and full of her experiences during the march-in. She had long had a passion for guideless travel in unknown places, and she found that each new area she visited affected her differently. For example, the Argentine Andes had cast her into the deepest despair, whilst the harsh Hindu Kush had the effect of strengthening her self confidence and courage. The Solo Khumbu obviously bestowed a cheerful serenity upon her.

"Here one's life and experiences are so intense; one doesn't just belong, one is part of the landscape. The unhurried pace is easily accepted. In Europe I couldn't wait to see you again. I was so impatient and edgy. But in Nepal as each day passed, I became more relaxed. I just kept going and going, looking at everything and drinking it all in. I have talked with the people and drunk tea in their houses. In Tengpoche we stayed an extra day simply because it was so beautiful. It was suddenly not so important whether I met you today or tomorrow, and so perhaps my joy in finding you is more than those heady days in Europe."

Everything that Uschi did, she did with such warmth and enthusiasm. Later, even our Sherpas, experienced in the ways of expeditions, were filled with admiration. She found the way, looked for camp sites, bought potatoes, chang and eggs. At home in South Tyrol we used to drink wine, here she supped the local brew, Rakshi, a greenish-white rice beer like a light schnaps. She would also eat Sherpa fare, and enquire how the dishes were made.

When we climbed up to Base Camp the next day, we secretly hoped that the face would have been cleared already and we could continue with our rambles through the Solo Khumbu. Uschi rolled up her blue jeans. Now and then the path became so narrow that we had to balance along it; she was good at this and always, when she didn't know where to go next, she turned round to me and smiled. Once she stopped to take off her sweater. It was very sultry and we had been on the go all day.

In the morning the Lhotse wall had reared high above us, wide and massive. From the Nuptse summit to Lhotse Shar must have been almost 10 kilometres, with an average height from base to summit of 3,000 metres. It was an enormous and menacing facade. Its appearance had quite changed since we first saw it; there were no longer any black rock buttresses, no ledges, no niches – now everything was white, the rock was verglased and snow covered the bands and terraces. Only the three secondary ridges which projected vertically from the wall into the valley, showed patches of brown – in places covered with smutty snow. Between these promontories, one saw the dead glaciers: the

Nuptse Glacier to the left, the Lhotse Glacier to the right. We had to pass to the left of them to climb up to Base Camp.

By the afternoon the features of the face, its ramps and ribs, were lost in turbulent cloud. In the continual shrouding and unshrouding, the wall no longer boasted any fixed points; new surfaces were constantly revealed, then concealed. To the right and left of the summit extended long banners of cloud. For a brief moment one could pick out from the swirling mist, two dots on the left hand side of the Ramp. Could these be the tents of Camp III, Uschi wanted to know.

"No, they are two rock spurs, each a hundred metres high. You wouldn't be able to see the tents even if you were standing in the middle of the Nuptse Glacier."

Later the cloud rolled across the face altogether, hiding it behind a snowstorm.

We were given a tremendous welcome when we arrived in camp. The men had been anxiously waiting to see the girls for many weeks and now they were at last here. They all knew Uschi already, they had met her during the preparations and at Milan Airport when we came away, but of the other two – Heidi and Inge – they only had hearsay to go on. They pressed around to greet them. Cassin, in particular, took a sympathetic interest while I led Uschi to my little tent. After a few hours the three girls had been accepted as part of the team.

During the long evenings they sat with us in our Night Club, talking and listening to our bawdy songs. They didn't understand them all, for our language had deteriorated daily since our failure, and it seemed almost as if we now had to prove that our manhood was not in question.

Uschi and I were often the subjects for good-humoured banter. Many lusty jokes were cracked at our expense, but I soon realised these were the produce of a certain envy on the part of the others. I asked myself from time to time, why they hadn't invited their wives or girlfriends to come along, and one evening as we talked in Piussi's tent, he said he was sorry he had not taken advantage of such a possibility.

"Next time I'll bring my wife along, then we can go for walks here too."

"No more expeditions without Uschi." So I promised her. In future she must be with me from the beginning like in 1971 on Mt. Kenya, 1972 on Noshaq, 1974 on Aconcagua.

That evening we were at our most relaxed; how could it be otherwise? We joked about the resolutions of the others, only to take part in mixed expeditions. For in truth Italian girls are home-loving creatures and happy to leave expeditions to the menfolk. Climbing is a game for hard men and, whosoever can stick it out – without women – is a real man indeed.

On the next day Sandro and I, together with a few Sherpas, were to climb the face to dismantle the high camps. With the same easy energy that had characterised him during the whole expedition, Sandro eagerly prepared for the last climb. With his slender, dexterous hands, he stuffed his equipment into his rucksack, took his exposed film from his camera and put it into a box. Two of the others tried to draw him into conversation.

"You won't get further than Camp I."

"Then we'll just have to clear Camp I" was his laconic reply.

One of the wounded Sherpas, who still bore bandages around his head and knee, remarked on the atrocious weather. Sandro answered him briefly, requested a sip of tea and picked up his rucksack.

"Ciao!" A nod to the Sherpas and off they went.

Meanwhile I was ready too. Slowly I began to climb to the moraine, and stumbled over the scattered stones beneath the wall. To start with I could not get any rhythm going; first I was too hot, then my right boot began to pinch. When at last I got into the swing of it, I found it difficult not to keep turning round to see if Uschi was still waving. Finally, my attention settled on the fixed rope, which had become buried in snow or hung encased in ice. About halfway up to Camp I, I had found my form and climbed steadily.

Suddenly I became obsessed with the idea that we hadn't really stretched ourselves on this expedition. We hadn't even once reached the ridge. But hang on – what had I to be ashamed of? For a minute I paused on the fixed rope, leaning back and looking up at the ridge, still clad in thick cloud. I recalled our last attempt when Mario Curnis and I set out to reach the summit ridge from Camp III. Everything had been well organised and we were in the best condition, but the rock we found there, was so fearfully bad and the wind roared incessantly. I thought of the easier snow slopes on the North side of Lhotse and of the possibility of climbing from the ridge to the summit in a single day. But we had not got as far as the ridge. The rock was so friable it had made the whole enterprise too dangerous. There was nothing we had left untried, and yet the feeling grew with each step, we had bungled it somehow.

Now, climbing quickly upwards, it struck me that just a few days of supreme effort would have been enough – taking into account, natur- ally, the risks that accompany a lightning attempt. So we had failed. But no-one had paid with his life.

What did it mean, mean to me, that the summit was not gained? No third eight-thousander – that was not so bad in itself, but not to have pushed the effort to a conclusion, that was the rub. I like tidy endings: I'm that kind of fool. I smiled and grasped the rope tightly again.

With my right hand I pushed the jumar clamp upwards, with the left, balanced myself against the rock. Meanwhile I made a few calculations and was delighted to find that it hadn't taken an hour to reach the first camp from Base. I felt as if my muscles were being pumped up like a football. There was a prickling sensation in my calves and thighs. Something urged me on, rather than to wait here for Sandro as I had previously resolved to do. I began to wonder if I could maintain this pace all the way to the top of the rope railway at 6,400 metres. Were the Sherpas already ahead of me? Had I reached the place where I had left my crampons hanging. My heart was beating violently. I climbed almost automatically, found the crampons, put them on, stood up and regained my tempo from peg to peg. A few moments later I caught up with the Sherpas who had left Camp I six hours before to get to the ropeway terminus by evening. I climbed past them and hurried on.

It was a good hour before Sandro joined me at the ropeway camp. I had made the tea by then and operated the winch. I had also set off in the direction of Camp II, but found the snow lying so deep that after a few steps I knew it would be doubtful if I could reach it that day, taking into consideration the seriousness of the climb. Also by now, after a short rest in the tent – I had grown very tired. I was now as exhausted as earlier I had been brimming with energy.

The next morning when we were ploughing up the last few metres of thick snow to Camp II, the buzzing of a helicopter disturbed the icy stillness. Our eyes followed the machine past the Nuptse Wall until it was a tiny black dot behind the West Ridge.

It took 3 hours to dig out the tents, oxygen cylinders, the radio, and to salve what fixed ropes we could. The Sherpas carried all our gleanings down to the cable-way, and from there we let it down in bundles – Wheee-bham! 400 metres in height on 600 metres of rope. The packets plumped into the snow like dud bombs.

As soon as we had all the men and materials back in Base Camp, we had only to pay off the Sherpas and to pack. Then we were free. Cassin undertook to lead the column of porters down the valley, leaving us to make our own way, and in Namche Bazar we would all meet up.

INTERLUDE

WANDERING THROUGH
SHERPALAND

Just a short while ago, I thought, we were mountaineers on an expedition, and now – Uschi, the two girls and I – were trekkers, ordinary ramblers. Simply to wander without porter worries, without haste, has its own advantages.

On the first day we went as far as the monastery in Tengpoche. In one of the guest rooms, situated in a side wing of the building, we were given an evening meal and space on a simple plank bed. There were other trekkers present, as well as two lamas who were selling beer and Tibetan trinkets, along with a few Nepalese who had been with the British Expedition to Nuptse and were now making their way home from resthouse to resthouse.

The shock of their terrible avalanche was with them still, and they had obviously been drinking Rakshi all evening. One of them even tried to snuggle up with me, but I was in no mood for jokes. About midnight we were awakened by a loud shouting. It was one of the Nepalese, a Gurkha, sounding off about Europe, – or at least, about the Europe of his imagination, which he claimed to know 'from London to Rome' – and about the expedition in which he had just taken part. "That bunch of morons" as he put it, "are scared to be left alone."

And suddenly we realised that the Nepalese – or at least, some of them – had a very different opinion of us than we, in our innocence, supposed; it was just that they managed mostly to conceal their hostility and aggression towards us. This man at all events hated Europe and expressed his hatred with just such scurrilous insults as he had learned from the Europeans themselves.

The Tengpoche monastery, called Gomba in the Sherpa tongue, was built a little over fifty years ago, and is the spiritual centre of Sherpa lamaism. It lies on a high plateau, that rises like a green island before the ridge of holy mountains – Ama Dablam, Kantega and Tamserku – and affords the most magnificent view of Lhotse and Everest. The building itself rests storey upon storey, each of its pagoda-type roofs seeming to support the one above. The walls, all spotted with mud, were painted in a Pompeiian red. The facade was symmetrically broken by windows in intricately-carved, brightly-painted frames, the wood seasoned to black by the sun. In front of the monastery high stone walls enclosed a courtyard. Steep steps led up to a carved door, and through the doorway one came to the courtyard, cloisters and the smokey kitchen in a side wing. The monastery itself contained a number of the most beautiful Thangkas – Tibetan scroll paintings, sacred images of the various manifestations of the deities, whose attributes one must seek to emulate through meditation – priceless Buddhas in gold and silver, as well as murals illustrating the life of Buddha. This for me, was one of the most beautiful places in the world.

Immediately below the monastery we crossed a rhododendron wood. The heavy scent of their dying blossoms hung in the air. Their petals ranged in colour from white, through yellow, to dark red; among the golden tones, it was the orange that predominated; the white was sometimes speckled with rose, sometimes as pure as fresh snow, and in between an infinite combination of reds on white.

Our way led past Khumjung and Kunde, the largest Sherpa settlement. We wanted to go to Thame where the greatest religious festival of the year, Mani Rimdu, was about to take place. Everywhere in the villages children ran after us, boys playing by the roadside, little girls carrying dolls on their backs in shoulder-cloths, just like their mothers carried the babies. Uschi liked to stop and talk to the children. Once, as she leant for a moment against a wall to rest, two small boys and a little girl came and sat next to her, trying to catch hold of her hands. Uschi's expression immediately changed. A hint of melancholy, an echo of sadness, crossed her face. I was reminded at once of my dream – of the hotel lobby the Kirchner print and the woman searching – Uschi was, as I suspected at the time, that woman. There is no escape from one's destiny.

Early in the morning we left the resthouse in Kunde, where we had spent the night not far from the Hillary Hospital. Passing through dense pinewoods and steep pastures, we took the road to Thame.

It was oppressively hot. Leaden clouds came right down to the foot of the mountains, and only now and then, did a patch of sunlight catch the stone walls around the fields. At last we reached Thame. The village seemed deserted, but far above, around the monastery, there was plenty of activity. Visitors had been streaming in for days to take part in the great festival. The monastery and its outbuildings were packed, and the Gomba full of visiting lamas from other monasteries.

The faithful had come together from the farthest corners of Sherpaland. Men, women, children and some foreign visitors mingled in a colourful throng. The resthouses were overflowing, young and old gathered around the field kitchens. It seemed more like an annual market with its antique dealers and chang sellers.

Faces I knew would appear in the crowd: two Sherpas who had

come as far as Camp III with me on Makalu, a camp that had projected like a springboard from the 60° ice slope; some climbers and trekkers I had met at lectures in Europe. A quick nod to the Sahibs, a 'Numaste' ('I greet the godliness in you') to the Sherpas.

As was customary, before the main festival began, the Ringpoche opened the proceedings. A bell rang and the whole monastery courtyard ceased its murmurings and expectant chatter, and sank into deepest silence.

The next morning there were more prayers and meditation for the pilgrims. A tarpaulin had been stretched from the eaves of the Gomba to cover the whole courtyard. Under it, on his throne-like seat, sat the Ringpoche, in the lotus position. He wore the high red hat of his order and a saffron silken robe. On an equally high seat to his right stood an ornamented portrait of the Dalai Lama. Other lamas occupied more lowly seats on either side of the Ringpoche.

On a table in front of him lay the most important cultural symbols of lamaism – Dorje, the sceptre, and Drilbu, the bell. From time to time the Ringpoche took up one or other of these implements, ringing the bell or raising the sceptre. He was a young man of about 17 and had come to this high office when it was recognised that he was the reincarnation of the lama priest who had led the monastery before him.

The high spot of the celebrations was the arrival of the masked dancers. Frequently changing their masks and robes, the lamas stepped out of the Gomba and danced, played music and recited, and it seemed as if all the music and movement and song united into a single entity. The symbolic and timeless world of these monks held us enthralled and filled us with a host of visions, sounds and scents.

On the evening after the festivities, we were allowed into the Gomba. Now the Ringpoche was no longer the remote high priest, but spoke with us and showed us an iron bar, a metre long and as thick as a man's finger. In one of his former incarnations he had twisted it into a knot without heating it, and this was a sign of his divinity.

Despite his youth, he radiated serenity and dignity. He showed us his private apartments and asked if we could mend his portable radio. Even here, in this last oasis of calm, technology has a hold, despite the fact that time is still measured by the rising and setting of moon and sun.

Uschi and I were in the highest of spirits all the way from Thame on the long march back to Namche Bazar. Although she was tired from the dusty journey and the sleepless nights in cramped, bug-ridden cells, nothing ruffled Uschi's good humour as we wound down the last hairpins of road into Namche Bazar.

Cassin was already there, and the greater part of the baggage – 300 pieces with porters and yaks – was well on its way to Lukla.

WAITING FOR THE HERCULES

"Campo base, campo due."

Loud laughter.

"Tutto bene, pico bello, Mamma mia, pasta asciutta."

A dark form was silhouetted against the flickering firelight, bandy-legged, feet turned out, and clasping a piece of wood in his right hand. Even the voice and intonation were those of the Old Man.

"Pronto, pronto, campo base."

One of the Sherpas was mimicking Cassin with his radio. He was so lifelike, that we too had to laugh. For a few moments I was right back in Base Camp.

Night had fallen and one of the Sherpas had invited us into his house. We sat there with the porters until well after midnight, drinking rakshi and chang, amid dancing, singing and laughter. Another Sherpa picked up the piece of wood and adopted Cassin's unique stance.

"Tutto bene?"

How well they had observed him! Before we left, they begged us not to tell the 'Bara Sahib', the Great White Chief, as they called him.

Every shade of colour from yellow to blue-green could be seen in the fields and woods the next morning. The young wheat sprouting on the terrace was a coppery-green, the ripe barley above, a warm gold, and between them the lichen-coloured wall, like a band of seaweed. The forest stretching to the horizon was a dusty grey-green, darker underneath, whilst in the undergrowth a splash of blue tint was seen whenever the sun disappeared behind a cloud. From a distance it seemed that the colour of the lower stems of the trees passed without gradation into the pastures beyond the cellular stone walls. Yet when one came close, a myriad colours were to be seen – the sulphurous yellow of the lichens growing on the bark to the dull corn-gold of the dried clumps of grass at the wood's edge. In the shadow of a Mani Wall I waited for Uschi and her sister. It was now only half an hour's walk into Lukla, from where the next morning, we would fly to Katmandu.

In part perhaps because of the leisurely walk back and the presence of Uschi, I now saw things in a different perspective, and had decided to take up the permit to attempt Hidden Peak. I hoped, therefore, to get to Europe quickly in order to prepare for this next expedition. But we were held up for two weeks in Katmandu. It was long past the date when, by our reckoning, the military aircraft should have picked us up. All we wanted now was to get home, and some of us were gradually losing patience.

In the meantime, I had been trying in vain to get the Ministry for Tourism in Rawalpindi, on the telephone. It was hopeless. Ever since the 1971 Indo-Pakistan War, all telephone communications were routed through London and it was very rare to get through. Neither did any of the telegrams I sent, concerning plans for my new expedition, bring any answers. In the ordinary way, I would have happily filled my days visiting temples and buddhas, but now I was like a caged beast. Every day that I idled here, could result in failure on Hidden Peak.

At last on 7th June, they announced the arrival of a Hercules aircraft; it had taken three weeks to get permission to fly over Indian territory. It seemed to us as if it had brought in half the Italian Alpine Club to meet us; half a dozen officials, their wives, journalists, friends. Surrounded now by his acquaintances and subjected to a volley of penetrating questions from the reporters, Cassin's failure suddenly came home to him. Always before he had returned home heaped with success, this time he was empty-handed.

To many of the questions, the Old Man's answers were terse; he growled and croaked like the Lhotse Face in a storm.

"Is it really impossible, this South Face?"

"Completely. Insurmountable. We gave up the direct line at first sight. The rock at the top is totally rotten, and down below the mountain is swept clean by falling stones and ice. When it snows, rivers of snow pour down the gullies, becoming uninterrupted avalanches lower down. There's no-one today who could climb that. Perhaps in 20 year's time someone might make it. Even then, he'd need an awful lot of luck. The Lhotse face isn't just two Eigerwands set one atop the other, it's a monster."

It had been Cassin who had dreamed up this expedition, who took the responsibility for it, and who, together with the President of CAI, Senator Spagnolli, got it off the ground.

This revered classical alpinist – possessed at the same time of both unbelievable integrity and inflexible stubbornness – was now a beaten man. His words, his whole attitude betrayed the personal drama he was going through. He could now see that patriotism and honour alone were not enough for an objective like the Lhotse Face, which was very different from climbing a high mountain by an easy route. For this, discipline and a scientific approach were needed, coupled with polished technique and a tenacity of will, given to very few men.

In his ill-humour, Cassin grumbled about the Sherpas, then withdrew into a surly silence. Though it was not his fault, the pain of disillusion nagged at him; failure was a new and ignoble experience.

"And what about Anghileri?" one reporter wanted to know.

"I put more trust in him than he deserved."

"But Anghileri has said you can't accuse someone of treachery, just because he doesn't want to stay with an outfit until he perishes. He rejects such traditional ethics. He says all these rules are made by the climbers themselves, and he laughed when, on his return, they threatened to expel him from the CAI. He says there's no virtue in suffering in silence; beyond a certain point, in fact, it's sheer masochism. He says anyone who claims he can only be happy in the mountains, is crazy. A climber can only be taken seriously if he remains true to his ideals, come what may."

Cassin remained silent. These were not the problems that had bothered him since Anghileri's departure. This man, to whom Italian alpinism owed such a debt, was no philosopher. So far as Anghileri was concerned, he saw himself as the father of the expedition, and had no comment to make on all these rationalisations.

During the impatient weeks of waiting, Uschi and I bought two puppies, two Lhasa Apsos, Tibetan monastery dogs. In the noisy, stripped-down military plane, they cowered in their basket, two woolly bundles no bigger than guinea pigs. Their eyes were wide with fear, but as soon as the engine started, they lay down on their backs, stretched out limply and remained thus until the plane finished its journey. We wondered at their ability to remain so completely relaxed, a trick they must have picked up from the Buddhist lamas who developed this ancient breed. On the journey home to Italy, we spoke a lot about Buddhism and the forbidden land of Tibet, the birthplace of our two young friends.

There was no great reception in Milan. A few friends were there. Aldo Anghileri, now patently not one of the team, and more journalists. For us everything seemed very simple and obvious. The Himalayas were no myth to us, Nepal not simply a land of dreams. Our expedition was a reflection of the times we live in; and journalists, steeped in the alpine literature of the fifties, found it difficult to understand us.

At last we caught a train to Bolzano, Uschi and I, with the holy dogs sitting up at the window, and the next morning we were home. It was

The rock pillar on the South Face of Lhotse above Camp I. The Sherpas refused to carry heavy loads up this section of the route. The Italians therefore constructed a rope railway between Camp I (6000m) and an intermediate camp at 6400m. This relieved the porters of a hard and difficult task.

June 13th. I had been away with the Lhotse expedition for three months. Now Hidden Peak beckoned and time was pressing.

I had already started making out cost estimates for the Hidden Peak Expedition in Katmandu on the way home from Lhotse. Including equipment, flights and all expedition costs, it all came to less than $8000.

5/6/75	Calculations. Lump Sum	approx. $
1.	RWP Hotel. $15 + $15 = $30 for 10 days.	300
2.	Tickets LO (Rps 164) RWP/SK Excess baggage (200-60 kg) + Rps 300.	100
3.	Royalty (Rps 9700 Bank cover)	1000
4.	General Exs. (Post and taxis)	100
5.	Purchase-Food. (340 + 40 + 350 + 90)	100
6.	Porters' insurance. Rps 1095.	100
7.	Porters' wages. 12 hrs. Rps 40 for 15 days.	720
	Two jeeps Skardu to Dassu 50 ml. × Rps, 10 × 2	90
8.	Liaison Officer. Food. (Rps 1800 in cash)	250
9.	Cooker and fuel.	50
10.	Porters' return march. 3 × 40 × 15	200
11.	Food, return journey. (eggs 1-2 Rps; Bread, Tea and apricots.	50
12.	Lodging RWP, homeward journey 3 × 30 max.	100
13.	General exs. return journey.	100
	Total exs. flights not included.	3260

Impressions of the return march from Lhotse to Katmandu.

THE DECISION

I was not able to get Peter Habeler on the telephone for some days.

"Perhaps it's better that way", I thought, after another morning spent unsuccessfully trying to get through, "that decides it once and for all." He was obviously not at home and I concluded that his original interest in Hidden Peak had evaporated owing to my very late return home.

I went out to Uschi in the garden and looked around for the dogs. We have a small but luxuriant flower garden round the south and east sides of the house. Uschi was straightening the bushes and pulling up weeds, which she tossed into a bucket. She tied the branches of a young plum tree to the wall of the house, and was visibly delighted with each new bud and blossom.

"This is going to be a good summer!" I said. "Next week I'll send off the manuscript for my mountain-people book, and then we'll be free to carry on with our own lives again."

I was glad Hidden Peak seemed off. Uschi and I would be able to do some climbing together, perhaps go for a whole week to Gschmagenhart – a farm at the foot of the Geislerspitzen – and get busy with the climbing school. Uschi, too, was looking forward to the peace and quiet of a summer together. We had never spent a spring together in Europe.

Then she went inside the house to get on with the meal, and I remained lying on the grass, playing with the dogs and leafing through the magazines that had come whilst I was away. After a while Uschi came out again, I could tell at once that she was having a struggle to hide her feelings. Her face betrayed a mixture of both disappointment and pleasure.

"That was Peter on the phone" she said lightly, "he's ready for anything."

She could easily see how quickly I picked up the whole Hidden Peak project again, with the same enthusiasm with which, a few

With only 12 Balti porters we marched more than 50km up the stone-covered Baltoro Glacier in heat and snow with vertical rock walls of up to 2000m to our right and left. In the background the elegant Trango Tower, a gigantic Guglia di Brenta.

St. Magdalena in the Villnöss Valley with the panorama of the Geislerspitzen. Here I live with my wife Uschi, a Persian cat and three Tibetan dogs in an old farmhouse which we fitted out ourselves.

moments before, I had been prepared to abandon it altogether.

"Of course you must go" she said, trying to be understanding, but at the same time, resigned.

She realised instinctively that to ask me not to go could only lead to friction, sooner or later I would regret it and feel I had been cheated out of something. If I was not to go, it had to be me who made the decision.

Peter arrived unexpectedly on the 20th June, bursting with enthusiasm. And when my friend Karl Vaja, President of the South Tyrol Provincial Assembly, offered to be patron of the expedition, and to give it his personal support, all thoughts I might have had of staying at home, went out of the window.

Poor Uschi! It wasn't just the restless life I led, but also that I left all my work at home for her to do. Even worse was the constant uncertainty – will he stay, or will he go? It was enough to make any woman despair.

Peter's enthusiasm was so infectious, it soon put to flight all my indecisions about whether I ought to go or not, which had been getting me down more than I cared to admit. I was now able and happy to focus all my attention on this Karakoram enterprise, and everything else was gradually pushed out of my mind. I felt joy, and at the same time, a thrill of anticipation.

Under a pile of post, I found a copy of a letter to Peter Habeler from the Styrian mountaineer, Hans Schell, from Graz.

"Dear Herr Habeler!

Edi Koblmüller has just rung me to say that you and Reinhold Messner have been granted permission to attempt Hidden Peak. Reinhold told me last year that he would like to try one of the eight-thousanders by a difficult route, as a party of two.

For a long time, we have planned an expedition to the Baltoro, but unfortunately I learned too late that the Pakistan authorities were once more allowing expeditions into the area, and so I was late putting in my application for a permit. We had principally wanted to climb Hidden Peak, but of the nine alternatives I put down, we have only received permission for Baltoro Kangri I.

I am writing to ask a big favour. Would you agree to the possibility of our combining forces and applying to the Pakistan authorities as a single expedition? I am assuming that you will be trying the Northwest Ridge, or one of the other difficult routes. As we only had plans to climb the ordinary, IHE Spur, route, we would be right out of your way, and would, in no manner diminish the importance of your two-man undertaking.

If the authorities are prepared to view us as a single expedition, we would of course meet the cost of the permit, and the expenses of the liaison officer. And if you haven't got a doctor, we could be of help there too.

Even if they did not see the undertaking as a single unit, they would grant us permission too if you had nothing against it.

If you want to, you could do a complete traverse of the mountain relatively easily.

I write to you because I don't know if Reinhold is back in Europe yet. We are going to leave Europe on June 7th, and on the 14th or 15th assemble in Rawalpindi.

Altogether we are six climbers, and would be extremely pleased to be able to climb Hidden Peak.

> *Thanking you in advance,*
> *With friendly greetings,*
> *Hans Schell."*

"Well it would get round the problem of the liaison officer," I said to Peter, "which I've always found to be one of the biggest nuisances."

"It would help with the finance, too."

This was quite a consideration. We needed to find about three or four thousand dollars, and were both in financial straits – Peter had been training intensively in preparation for Hidden Peak, and had not been working, and I had been away for five months on Lhotse with no regular income.

In the main we were financing this expedition ourselves, and any other money we got was from private sources. Some articles for a paper and a television appearance yielded a bit, and we received modest grants from the Alpine Club and the North Tyrol Government.

"If Schell is waiting in Rawalpindi, and ready to pay for the permit and the liason officer, he can climb the ordinary route for all I'm concerned; he won't disturb our plans", said Peter. "But we must make it known beforehand, for the alpine historians will be watching us like hawks:"

I sent off a telegram to the Ministry of Tourism in Islamabad, Rawalpindi:

"Arrival of Tyrolian Karakorum Expedition Hidden Peak in two weeks. Give notice to Hans Schell, leader of Baltoro Kangri I immediately, telling him he can share in our expedition. I expect answer by Schell immediately. Messner, Tyrolian Karakorum Expedition."

Upon their reply would depend whether we co-operated or not. Schell should be there already, and would be informed of our arrival.

Realising that my decision was now final, Uschi busied herself the next morning with preparations for the expedition. Although it was not yet certain whether we would fly out on the Tuesday or the Wednesday of the following week, as we had not heard from the Pakistan International Airlines in Frankfurt, she set off the same morning to Bressanone to take care of the most important purchases.

That evening she asked me to go for a walk with her round the church, a favourite stroll of ours. We usually let the dogs have a run whilst we sat on the bench by the churchyard wall and chatted. We walked slowly along the narrow, gravel path. It was not that I was completely immersed in the plans for the new expedition – it was still too early for the finer organisational problems that were bound to crop up – but I was busily adjusting to my suddenly altered situation.

"If you had to choose", Uschi asked me at length, after we had been sitting silently side by side, "choose between the mountains or me – which would it be?"

"You're not seriously asking such a question?"

92

"I have asked it."

I remained silent. What could I say? What could I say at this moment.

"When you're away," she continued, "you write such long, yearning letters, saying how much you miss me, then after two weeks back home, you are already off again."

After another pause, she added, "It's all just so many words. You don't mean it."

She had a point. How often had I sworn never to go on another big journey without her. In all the high camps, during the long weeks of marching in, in faraway towns, I had said it, again and again. But this was different. The trip to Hidden Peak would be too dangerous, and besides, Peter and I wanted to do this one alone, an eight-thousander in a two-man party.

I had a camera session the following afternoon with Luis Trenker, an interview with the theme 'Fifty Years on the Furchetta North Face'. We finished in half an hour, and afterwards Luis, a skilled raconteur, sat for several hours in our garden, entertaining everybody – cameramen, producer, sound technicians. Later on, Peter Habeler and Karl Vaja joined us too. Trenker, who in 1913 had made the first ascent of the 800 metre perpendicular Furchetta Wall with Hans Dülfer, simply oozed charm and vitality. He displayed a lively interest in our project, as well as for the situation of the Villnöss hill farmers, and he regaled us with colourful episodes from his own life.

After Uschi had seen our guests to the door, she turned back into the living room, but instead of sitting down, began restlessly pacing up and down. She no longer seemed to approve of my action. Although throughout the afternoon and evening, she had been using all her powers of persuasion to win our friends and guests over to my new expedition, and although she perceived she had been successful in this, she was now displeased with both herself and me.

"You are slowly destroying me, you know", she complained.

"I love you."

"When you're there, you want me, want to take utter possession of me, but when you're away, you just leave me with my grief and all *your* work and problems. No wife can take that indefinitely."

Again she was right. But although I could see that I was paying her too little attention, I could not give up this particular challenge. The plans must stand. Afterwards, I would live only for her.

"Afterwards! I've heard that before. Then comes the big pay off! And what do we get? Lectures, a book perhaps, and then, beyond any doubt, some other plan."

She was in despair. What could I do to comfort her?

93

Peter's life, in the meantime was equally full of work and commitments that left him no time for anything else. After the completion of the ski instructors' courses, which as Chief Instructor of the Austrian Mountain Guides Association, he was obliged to attend, he was busy lecturing and then travelled to Bolzano to meet Tiziana Weiss. This young lady from Trieste, the home of Emilio Comici, was a climbing phenomenon, who had made a name for herself during the last few years with some major routes, especially in the Dolomites. Peter had met her at the Trento Festival, when they had done a few climbs together. At the same time, he promised to introduce her to the Wilder Kaiser in the spring. Now they went together to Ellmau and during an ascent of the Mauk West Face, something happened, which upsets him as much today as it did then. They were climbing the upper part of the route, the major difficulties behind them, when Peter, who knew the climb of old, suddenly fell off backwards when a hold came away in his hand. Tiziana had not got him securely belayed and couldn't arrest him; Peter fell seemingly for ever into the void. Then when he was about thirty metres below her stance, the rope got caught up in her legs. Peter was swinging like a pendulum against an overhanging section. The girl could neither haul him up, nor render him any assistance. With commendable presence of mind, Peter managed to swing across to the Mauk Spur; he climbed up it, without any karabiners or fifis, and traversed back across to his original stance. Tiziana was not a little astonished, when he suddenly reappeared close by. She had supposed him to be dangling beneath her and probably suffocating to death, certainly no longer in a position to help himself, and there he was, coming down from above. The incident had only lasted a few minutes, but it had made a great impression on Peter and he kept harking back to it. It had only happened because he knew the climb so well that, without first testing it, he had trusted his whole weight to a single large jug-hold, which he had always considered to be safe.

A few days before our departure for Hidden Peak, I sent a telegram to Pakistan, to the Foreign Ministry, to say we would be arriving in Rawalpindi on the 4th July. The telegram was also intended to acquaint Hans Schell of our plans. I rather hoped that one of his party would be waiting for us in Rawalpindi, and that we could unite our two expeditions somehow for the march in.

Uschi and I in the meantime, had split up the work between us. She took care of the shopping in Bressanone, whilst I stayed at home packing, planning and making out lots of lists. At the most, all the time we had together was a few minutes in the evening, when we would chat or go for a short stroll. I could see that amid this hectic activity, she was

Peter Habeler, climber and ski instructor, is one of the best mountaineers in the world. An elegant rock climber, quick and competent on any terrain, acclimatises well.

still very distressed, and I could understand it. I was not entirely happy in my own mind about my decision, especially after promising only a week before, that I would stay home for the summer. But the prospect of this unique chance to launch a two-man attack on an eight-thousander, and the possibility at the same time, of bagging my third eight-thousander, pushed the other considerations from my mind.

Two days later, Uschi and I went to Innsbruck to meet Peter. We had a frightful scramble – photos to be collected, and a picture that Walter Spitzstatter, an extreme climber from Innsbruck, was reproducing for us to use as a post-card. It showed Hidden Peak from the Abruzzi Glacier. We needed to buy clothing, and finally had to dash to the Austrian television studios for an interview with Manfred Gabrieli, who was always interested in mountaineers and their plans.

There wasn't much time for a cosy get-together. All we could manage was a cup of coffee before Peter went back to the Zillertal, and Uschi and I to South Tyrol. When we did talk, it was exclusively about the expedition – money difficulties; equipment still to buy; food, which we hadn't done anything about yet. Also we needed some maps and ridge sketches of the Karakorum.

95

As we travelled back over the Brenner Pass, Uschi and I began a serious talk.

"Not even time to drink a cup of coffee in peace", she complained.

"Forgive me", was all I could say.

"It's nothing. You are away the whole year and in between, when you come home for a couple of months, or even only for a couple of weeks, all your thoughts are about packing, new books you're going to write, or the expedition you will make next year or the year after."

"But this is a very special opportunity – you know that jolly well. You yourself agreed."

"What do you mean 'special opportunity'? All your opportunities are special. What about Everest in 1978?"

"But we're just about to go. We've got to plan and discuss the final details. Any little thing we forget now, could spell failure later on."

"I know, I know. Mountains are your life, your be-all and end-all."

"No, that's not true. Mountains are not my *whole* life, but they are a fascination. The chance to go to an eight-thousander is something I can't resist, or a mountain in the Western Alps, either – like the Matterhorn, for instance."

"I can understand that. But why does it have to be *this* summer, when you've only just got home?"

"Because the permit's for this summer. It's not something that happens every day – I might never get sanction for a climb like this again. It really is *the* big chance. Truly."

"I do understand, but we might at least have made time for a quiet cup of coffee together!"

Uschi insisted on her coffee, and I understood her argument only too well. She was dead right. I was being selfish. It was unfair. I only had time and energy for my new ambition and all my enthusiasm was directed towards that.

When we got up the next morning Uschi volunteered to go down to Bressanone for the umpteenth time to buy the last items of food for the expedition. Without her help, this trip would never have got off the ground. And it wasn't just that she helped, but that she was right behind me in my plan, even though she didn't fully agree with it, and even though she was miserable at the thought of being alone again for months on end.

On this particular morning, a number of journalists from South Tyrol Television called on me again, and I was subjected to another barrage of questions.

"Is it possible that Hidden Peak could be climbed by just two people? An eight-thousander without oxygen, without high camps, without porters?"

"Theoretically, yes. Absolutely."

When I was asked what our chances were of reaching the top, I said with conviction:

"Fifty-fifty. We could get up, or not. It depends on the weather, and of course, not least on our own physical condition; whether or not one of us gets sick, or our equipment isn't up to the job."

To keep the expedition costs down, we were not taking spares of everything.

By midday on June 30th, everything was ready. In between the packing, I had made telephone calls, given another television interview and concluded the most urgent work, and now I stood amidst the bags and boxes, all packed up and ready to leave the next morning.

My last night at home. Long silences, interspersed with a few words, and an underlying anxiety. Will everything go all right? Will we make it? But it was not the fear of a condemned man, nor of a soldier before battle. It was merely an uncertainty that kept working up into a fear, and then fading again whenever Uschi said something. Had it been possible for her to come with us, I am sure this uncertainty would never have arisen.

After Uschi had gone to sleep, I lay there and went over in my mind all the difficulties I had encountered on earlier expeditions: the retreat from Makalu; the failure on Lhotse. It was madness, what we were now intending. To calm myself, I checked through all the details: equipment – we had the lightest there was; Peter – a better partner you couldn't hope to find. He was fast, strong and reliable, one of the best climbers in the world. A trifle intense perhaps, but always completely calm in a crisis. Self-confident, without being a hot-head. Dependable, not tall, lean, completely in training to the last fibre, physically ideal for an eight-thousander. He had successfully completed all his big climbs, he always came through, he had an urge to succeed. He had been in crisis situations – although never as high as 8,000 metres, but on high mountains all the same. He had never experienced the 'Death Zone', but was fully prepared for it.

Turning these thoughts over in my mind, must have eventually sent me off to sleep. By morning I was much calmer, and my confidence had returned. Uschi slipped out of bed before me and was already in the kitchen. What had been the cause of my apprehensions the night before? As I washed and dressed, I thought about it. Was it the experience of earlier expeditions, the knowledge of what could possibly crop up? With less experience, would I worry correspondingly less? How important was a man's life anyway? My life?

The boxes were all standing packed by the door, and an hour later

Shortly before leaving for Hidden Peak, I did my usual training runs in Villnöss and from Bolzano to S. Genesio. I was glad to be able to record 1000m up hill in 35 minutes. My self confidence increased in spite of days spent hard at work at my desk, organising the expeditions and sitting in my car, I was in fine form.

when Karl Vaja appeared, the last bits and pieces that Uschi had bought, were all stowed away. We put two of the boxes into Karl's car and one into our VW, and in the afternoon set off for Innsbruck and Mayrhofen, where there was to be a farewell party for us, organised by the Mayor of Mayrhofen.

In spite of the rain, a lot of people had turned out. There was a gay atmosphere. Our expedition was still provoking a lot of discussion and argument. I knew of the misgivings many other climbers felt, but I still believed that we had as much chance as a larger expedition. I hadn't had much success in convincing other people of this. The band played; the Mayor made a speech, and so, of course, did our friend Karl, who was present both in his capacity as our patron and as an official representative of the South Tyrol Government. Wolf Girardi brought greetings from the North Tyrol authorities, and Luis Lechner, Youth Leader of the Austrian Alpine Club, a very old friend of Peter and I, the best wishes of the OAV for our success.

What especially pleased us was that Hias Rebitsch had come along, a veteran expedition-mountaineer, who was the first man to return alive from an attempt on the North Wall of the Eiger. Hias has had a lot of bad luck during his own climbing career, and was as dubious about our chances as the others, but at least he trusted us to come back safe and sound.

We sat late that night talking with our particular friends, the Spieszens. Above all, in this narrow circle of climbing guides and friends, we encountered the encouragement and moral support that gave us the impetus to carry our plan through. Later on, after everyone else had gone to bed, Uschi and I were left alone and stood a long time on the balcony of the Pension Kumbichl, talking things over. All she said rolled off me; I was not listening; my thoughts were already far away, already in Pakistan. If I sensed the impending loneliness, into which I had voluntarily committed myself, at all, it was completely overshadowed by my excitement over the prospect of our challenge.

The next morning, Uschi, still half-dressed, stepped out onto the balcony again. From her expression and movements I could see how miserable she was, and wanted to say something. But I just couldn't find the right words with which to comfort her. My wife, who knew and hated my habit of repeatedly looking at my watch in such situations, just stared at me dumbly. And that was far worse than if she had ranted at me. Silently I collected my things together. I didn't stop to think whether or not we had time to have breakfast together at least. It seemed that I was only able to think a few moments ahead at a time, and then purely in a mechanical and superficial fashion. This was July 2nd. We left that morning for Munich. Uschi and I quickly went to the PIA Office to pick up the flight tickets. From there we raced to the airport. We were already pressed for time as they had just announced our flight would be leaving early because of the delayed arrival of another service. I ripped the luggage out of the car, almost before we had stopped. Uschi ran after me with my rucksack. There were all sorts of acquaintances and journalists waiting in the lobby to see us off, but I saw everything in a haze and failed to greet them. I was in a kind of trance – flashbulbs, questions, a whirl of activity. At the weigh-in and luggage check, Gunther Sturm, head of the mountain and ski school of the German Alpine Club, helped us with our baggage – 160 kilos altogether. Messages and telephone numbers were stuffed into my hand which, when I rediscovered them two days later in my pocket, came as a surprise, as I had no recollection of being given them at all.

Thanks to understanding friends, who saw to the right things at the right time, we managed to make the flight.

In the hustle and bustle of the last few minutes, I had not had the opportunity to say goodbye to Uschi properly. I was pushed onto the plane, and it was only as I sat there that I realised with a shock that Uschi still had the tickets. A stewardess hurried off and asked for a few minute's delay. Uschi was paged and the tickets pushed through a crack in the door of the waiting lounge. Five minutes later the engines started and soon we were high in the air.

In Munich and Innsbruck climbers were laying bets that we would fail, or worse still, never come back. We were told that, of the many people who knew of our project and understood something of its nature, only two thought we had any chance of success. And only then, if we encountered more than our fair share of luck. There was a lot of argument about the audacity of our plans, and a lot of people felt that the most favourable time for an attempt was already past, that before we got to our mountain, the monsoon would have started. Some said we had not got a permit, others that Peter had insufficient high altitude training. In fact the air was full of rumours.

HIDDEN PEAK

THE FAREWELL THAT NEVER WAS

"He's gone! Flown off without a word, nothing!". Uschi ran distractedly about among her friends before she fully realised what had happened. "That was no sort of farewell", she said to herself, "but how can you say goodbye properly with all this razzamatazz."

She felt very upset about it, but would not allow herself to mope.

Peter and I landed in Frankfurt. Our PIA Cairo/Karachi flight had developed a fault, and nobody knew how long it would take to put right, so after all the hectic bustle of the previous days, we were now forced to wait idly, very much against our will. It was only when at last we sat back in the aircraft that I was able to relax and think about things in perspective. I was sorry to have had so little time for Uschi and not even to have been able to say goodbye. It came home to me with some force that Peter and I were launched on the biggest adventure possible in modern mountaineering, and we should be away for two or three months.

We had to wait some hours in Karachi. I spent the time reading and dozing, then the same night, we went on to Rawalpindi. The customs formalities presented no problems and soon we were installed in Flashman's Hotel, despite the early hour.

There was always plenty to do in Rawalpindi before an expedition – permits to see to and such – and all the time I kept thinking about when Uschi and I were here together a few years ago. Despite some new high-rise building and the garishly-painted buses, Rawalpindi could still not really be called a city. Its melancholy, slightly raffish, Moslem lifestyle, that I loved so much, hadn't changed. That first evening in Flashman's Hotel, I ordered the Chicken Kiev, all the time remembering when Uschi and I had sat and dined here in 1971 after our return, completely shattered, from Nanga Parbat. It had been our first brush with civilisation again after our months away, and it was here, after a thorough wash and de-lousing, we had once again to readjust to normal civilian existence.

Next morning Peter and I got in touch with the Ministry for Tourism to clarify the position over our permit and Hans Schell. Mr. Awan, the gentleman responsible, was not there and nobody else knew anything about our liaison officer. We refused to be put out by this waste of time. From my experience with oriental officialdom, I have learned to always allow plenty of time, so that the inevitable delays don't make me lose patience. The only thing we did learn was that the Graz party had already set out with neither a permit for Hidden Peak, nor having made arrangements for a combined liaison officer. Under these circumstances, we no longer felt we could let them climb Hidden Peak by the ordinary route. We were, in fact, resolved to prevent them doing so if at all possible.

On this particular afternoon we happened to meet Yannick Seigneur, a climbing guide from Chamonix, who had just climbed Gasherbrum II and was now staying in a simple hotel near us with his companions from this French expedition. His news from the Karakorum was not very encouraging. During their stay on the Baltoro Glacier, they had encountered a lot of snow and bad storms, besides having had trouble with their porters. His expedition had been dogged by bad luck. In the course of a second summit attempt, under Louis Audoubert, one of the team members perished in a blizzard; they retreated from the mountain under scorching skies, ploughing their way through deep snow and across raging glacier torrents. Now, physically and mentally burnt out after the days of anguish over their lost friend and the rigours of the expedition, they sat about abstractedly, their thoughts still back in that fateful snowstorm near the summit.

The tragedy that befell their expedition will be interpreted by some as a malignant quirk of fate, by others as the result of over-confidence. They had climbed Gasherbrum II by its West Ridge and launched a second bid when they were hit by a fearful storm. Seigneur, who had led the successful first rope, had already climbed down as far as Camp II, so Louis Audoubert was left alone in the bivouac with his companion, Villaret, who was suffering from altitude sickness. The hurricane raged for days with such violence that the two could not even open their tent door, and they had nothing to drink. Villaret deteriorated rapidly and was no longer capable of getting himself down without outside help. So Audoubert left the bivouac and crawled alone down through the storm to Camp II to fetch assistance. But it was already too late for Villaret. There was so much snow that to launch a rescue attempt from below seemed impossible. Some days later the party evacuated all camps and withdrew down the Baltoro Glacier. Nothing more was seen or heard of Villaret.

During the spring of 1975, every tenth man who took part in a large expedition to Nepal perished. And now another fatality on an eight-thousand metre peak. There was always this incalculable element of chance about a mountain of this height.

Yannick came back into the hotel lobby, bringing a sketch. With his

MERKZETTEL / 4. VII. 75

Abflug nach Skardu : ca. 48 Std. vorher melden
                                    bei MR. AWAN abmelden
Trekking Permit (6 × 2 Fotos) : Police Station
Träger-Versicherungen : Tel. 68349
                                    National Bank

ETAPPEN
Dassu - Paiju = 6 Tage   } min. 2 Wochen
Paiju - BC = 7/8 Tage   }

PREISE :
Jeeps : 9-12 Rps / km
Liaison Officer (L.O.) 60 Rps / Tag [Verpflegung]
Lohn Träger : 30 Rps / o   (in Askole Schuhe u.)
                 ohne Verpfl. (Verpflegung kontrollieren)

                 30 Rps   (? riskant > Streiks)
                 + Verpfleg.

Einkäufe
RWP : Öl (z. Kochen)   SKARDU : 1 Schaf
      Salz   Tee (ca. 4 Pakete)
      Milchpulver   Brennst. + Ofen
      Fleischkons.   Atta (Mehl)(für
      Zigaretten / Träger   Zucker (cooks)
      Zündhölzer   ASKOLE : Atta + Dall,
                                    Ghee (Butter)

This memorandum gradually increased in detail in Rawalpindi as a result of conversations with climbers back from the Karakorum.

MEMORANDUM   4/7/75.

Flight to Skardu. About 48 hrs. Report to Mr Awar. Trekking permit (6 × 2 photos): Police Station. Porters' insurance: Tel. 68349, National Bank.

DISTANCES.

Dassu to Paiju = 6 days   } minimum 14 days.
Paiju to Base Camp = 7-8 days. }

PRICES.

Jeeps: 9-12 Rps/km
Liaison Officer. 60 Rps/day (food)
Porters' wages. 30 Rps without food. (see to boots and food in Askole)
30 Rps + food (? risky - strikes)

PURCHASES

RWP	SKARDU.
Oil for cooker	1 sheep
Salt	tea (about 4 pkt)
Powdered milk	Fuel for cooker.
Preserved meats	atta (flour)
Cigarettes and matches for porters	sugar.

ASKOLE.

atta, dall and ghee (butter)

long blonde hair, his new beard and his blonde eyebrows, he looked very dashing. His tanned skin set off his striking features to advantage. He is reckoned as one of the best climbers in the world, and his ascent of Gasherbrum II was his second eight-thousander. There were, including himself, only four Sahibs to have twice climbed 8,000 metre peaks – Hermann Buhl with Nanga Parbat and Broad Peak; Kurt Diemberger with Broad Peak and Dhaulagiri I; then Seigneur with Makalu and Gasherbrum II, and myself with Nanga Parbat and Manaslu. A few months later Dougal Haston joined this select band when he reached the summit of Everest by its Southwest Face, having already climbed Annapurna.) There are also two Sherpas – Gyaltsen Norbu and Lakpa Tensing – who have twice stood on 8,000 metre summits, the first with Makalu and Manaslu, and the second, with Dhaulagiri I and Everest.

Who would be the first mountaineer to achieve success on three eight-thousanders? I knew that Yannick Seigneur was playing with the idea and had put in an application for an expedition to Broad Peak. But for the time being at least, he had had about enough. Nothing was as important to him at this moment as to get home as quickly as possible to his wife and child.

Now that Seigneur and his party had damped our enthusiasm somewhat, we were forced to recognise that half the success of our expedition would depend upon our reaching Base Camp safely.

BETWEEN RAWALPINDI
AND ISLAMABAD

Next morning Peter and I went again to the Tourist Ministry in Islamabad, a modern satellite town of Rawalpindi, in which all the government offices are situated. We met Mr. Awan, who gave us precedence over the other waiting expeditions – fortunately we had applied at the right time – and he proved extremely helpful. He promised that our liaison Officer would be ready for us on Monday 7th July and that everything else would be put in order without delay.

We met our French friends again in the afternoon. They gave us a few tips, like how and where to buy foodstuffs, where to get good porters and how best to handle them on the long trek to the Baltoro Glacier. And during the same afternoon, Peter and I put our heads together and discussed our finances. We still had 3,000 dollars or thereabouts, and that would have to do.

There were several other expeditions in the town at this time – a Swiss group heading for Tirich Mir and another team, also mostly Swiss, with Sia Kangri as their goal. Dölf Reist was with them and suggested we could march part of the way together.

In the meantime we had learned that the Schell party had left Skardu some days before. This was the last port of call for all Karakorum expeditions, and they must now be well on the long journey to Base Camp. We were now convinced that they had given up all ideas of a joint expedition and this was why they hadn't waited for us. We were sure they wouldn't be coming to Hidden Peak and had most probably reverted to their original objective, Baltoro Kangri I. So, for the time being, we gave the matter no further thought.

We got our hair cut in the Intercontinental Hotel at midday and afterwards lounged a long time by the swimming pool. In the evening we were considerably surprised to see Sandro and Ornella Gogna coming towards us. At the end of the Lhotse Expedition, the pair of them had travelled from Nepal to here in their VW bus. Even though Sandro had mentioned a possible meeting when we were both in Katmandu, I hadn't really expected it to come about.

Sandro lent us his bivouac tent, and we swapped some gas; he had a blend of propane and butane specially for altitude use, whilst we only had the normal gas which he said would suit him better in the heat of India. Soon we parted again with completely different, but equally interesting, prospects before us – he an overland journey to Italy, we an eight-thousander alpine-style.

We waited in vain the whole of the next morning for our liaison officer. Every expedition in Pakistan must take a liaison officer, and his equipment must be provided by the expedition. Fortunately, Peter and I had assembled the necessary equipment for such an officer whilst we were waiting fruitlessly for a reply from Hans Schell. As our officer had not turned up by the afternoon, I went back to Mr. Awan, and he promised that the man would certainly be there that evening, or the next morning at the latest.

And so he was. At 11 o'clock the next morning Captain Khaled presented himself to us, the third member of our party, who would accompany us as far as Base Camp. Khaled was tall, with black, curly hair and dark brown eyes. He must have been about 25 years old and he told us he had been training hard for this assignment – cross-country runs, sleeping in the open, forced marches. He was ambitious and self-confident and was obviously determined that all should go well. He promised to do his best for the expedition, and Peter and I could see right away that in him, we had been very lucky indeed. Together we worked out our timetable, then we all three hurried to the insurance office to take out accident cover for our valley porters, as required by the Pakistani authorities. Then to the Police for an extension to our visas. Then we checked over with Khaled the equipment we had brought for him. With the exception of the boots, which were far too small, he was delighted with it all. We searched around for hours in Rawalpindi without locating him any boots of the right size, so he promised to find some himself, which we would pay for.

So everything was settled, and over a cup of coffee in the Intercontinental, Peter and I reviewed the events of the last few days to make sure we hadn't forgotten anything. The permit had taken another 1,000 dollars from our funds; the additional food we had bought in Rawalpindi, was all packed. Now we were only waiting for the flight to Skardu. The route could only be flown in fine weather, and if one was unlucky, it was possible to have to wait for a long time.

I had just settled the bill, when through the window of the restaurant, I saw outside in the swimming pool of the hotel, a man I thought I knew. He was very sunburned, and as he dived in I glimpsed an ironical smile. It hit me like a bolt from the blue – Wackernell! As he surfaced I took another look. Was this really Engineer Wackernell, my former professor, on whose account I had had to sit my Abitur twice? I hurried to Reception and asked if a Herr Wackernell was checked in at the hotel, a

Khaled, our Liaison
Officer on Hidden
Peak was
sympathetic and
helpful.

Norbert Wackernell. They confirmed he was, and I ran out to the
swimming pool to speak to him. He recognised me and we both laughed
at this strange coincidence, meeting like this after ten years. We were
both genuinely pleased to see each other. But the evening brought
another surprise, and a very unhappy one for Peter and me. Our seat
reservations for Skardu appeared to have been inexplicably cancelled,
and we were now on a waiting list with thousands of others. I tackled
officials and flight personnel, trying first flattery, then abuse.

"We were booked on the next flight!"

"Maybe – but it's full."

"We've been waiting here for ten days. If we don't get away tomorrow, we shall be too late for our mountain."

Once more we came up against oriental bureacracy. One person sent
us to the next, and he in turn passed us to someone else. It was enough
to drive us crazy. In the East, there is always something new to learn
about patience. Shortly before the office closed, we had finally secured
three places on a flight the following morning, with a maximum allow-
ance of 200 kilograms of luggage. Quickly we packed again and re-
weighed our bags and boxes – 180 kilos all told. In the hope that we
would at last get away, we settled down to sleep.

As we waited hour after hour at the airport the next morning for our
flight to be called, I became increasingly convinced that we should never

get started. Then suddenly a Hercules came in from Gilgit, reawakening a glimmer of hope. Would this plane fly on to Skardu? We watched it carefully and I was surprised to see half a dozen climbers scrambling out. It was the Felix-Kuen-Memorial-Expedition, under the leadership of Dr. Herrligkoffer, on its way home, or at least it was a part of the team.

I hurried into the reception hall to speak to them and hear what had happened on Nanga Parbat. The first person I met was their liaison officer. He was surprised how much I knew about the mountain and told me that the expedition had attempted three separate routes – one to the left of the Rupal Flank, which looked ideal and had been tried before by Toni Kinshofer; then a bold line on the Southeast Ridge; and thirdly, the South Ridge of Rakhiot Peak, long but certainly interesting. From what he told me, I gathered that they had disseminated their energies too widely, coupled with the fact that the weather too had been very bad, so they were forced to turn back without making any attempt on the summit itself.

In the dusty baggage bay, Dr. Herrligkoffer, in his light tropical suit, hands deep in his pockets and his peaked cap at a crazy angle, strode up and down. Ten paces up, ten back. It had been five years since one of his expeditions had reached the summit of Nanga Parbat and he seemed tired. Morosely, he stared at the glass partition that separated the baggage bay from the reception hall. As I approached this screen, it seemed to me that he had recognised me. He stood still suddenly, stared, and then turned towards the door. Quite automatically, I followed on my side of the glass, and as we came towards each other, he held out his hand hesitantly, greeting first me and then Peter. We held an animated conversation on the subject of his expedition and the relative difficulties of the routes it attempted; much of the blame for the failure of the expedition could be put on the bad weather and the avalanches. Dr. Herrligkoffer praised his team, and the route they had managed to make up to the Mazeno Pass.

Then, a further wait, at last our flight was called and we ran out onto the runway, checked that our baggage was aboard, and were bitterly disappointed when it was suddenly announced that the flight had been cancelled.

"The weather is too bad; there will be no flight today", was the terse reply to our anxious enquiries.

Another valuable day lost. We were fast becoming dispirited for time was running out if we wanted to climb Hidden Peak. Back in the hotel, we had another brief chat with the Nanga Parbat people, who had also checked in at Flashman's. I was surprised to learn that the actions of my brother Gunther and me on the Nanga Parbat Expedition of 1970, was often held out to them as a worthy example.

Peter and I invited Mr. Awan out to dinner. We had a quiet smile to ourselves when we saw we had chosen the same place to eat as Dr. Herrligkoffer, who was dining with a rather pretty young lady and an eminent Pakistani. With them was Michl Anderl, who had been climbing leader of the 1970 expedition. This time, Dr. Herrligkoffer ignored us completely, in contrast to his earlier friendliness.

The next day we again waited three hours at the airport. Any hope that we would be able to get away seemed more remote than ever. A thick bank of storm clouds had built up in the north east, which seemed to seal off the way to Skardu like an impenetrable wall. The flight staff were in no hurry to load the machine. Peter, finding the heat and stink of the waiting room too much to bear, was lying outside on a small patch of grass, his rucksack under his head, his sun hat over his eyes, seemingly sleeping happily. But in truth he was getting quite agitated, worrying over our delay; he kept calculating and re-calculating the number of days we should need to reach Base Camp. Suppose there was a porter strike? A snow storm? A river in flood? He must allow for these. The more he pondered what in effect were imponderables, the further away our objective seemed.

I had another talk with the airport officials, keeping my eyes on our baggage all the time. The boxes, sacks, ice axes and pack frames were stacked in front of the waiting room, and Khaled, who was now lying down on the grass with Peter, had tied them all together with a piece of line. It all became too much – this waiting, this inactivity, the uncertainty – and I joined the others on the grass.

At last at 9 a.m. on July 12th, everything was ready. We could board a Pakistan Army Hercules, which held about fifty people and an enormous amount of luggage. Squeezed in between women and children, we sat with packets, baskets and boxes piled upon our feet. Right up to the last minute we dared not believe we were really away, but at last the engine sprang into life and we taxied down the runway. Only then was I sure our special expedition had begun.

WE LOSE OUR SENSE OF TIME

We flew in over the foothills, thick banks of cloud beneath us. I peered out intently, trying to see as far ahead as possible. Sooner or later Nanga Parbat should emerge on our right. The mountains were getting larger and lighter in colour by the minute. Then I suddenly saw it – Nanga from the southwest, with the Rupal Flank to the right and Diamir Flank to the left. I pointed out to Peter the route that Günther and I had taken five years ago in our desperate struggle to get off the mountain. This was a moving moment for me. As we flew past, I was able to pick out in detail each patch of rock and ice, each avalanche cone. Although it was difficult to see much out of the small windows of the Hercules, I recognised the various rock ribs and saw the scattered dwellings in the Diamir Valley. All too quickly we had left Nanga behind and were floating over the desolate valleys in the direction of Skardu.

A large number of climbers were waiting in Skardu for the return flight to Rawalpindi. Expeditions greeted one another, some on their way home, others setting out. Some French climbers were sitting there, all dirty, dishevelled and emaciated. They looked as if they had been lost in a desert for days; actually, they had been to Paiju Peak with Frehel, where they had met with no success and eventually become separated from the main party. They were now on their way home, fed-up to the teeth and cured of the Karakorum for ever. Some of them had fallen into a torrent and nearly drowned before their companions were able to pull them out in the nick of time.

I also noticed amongst those waiting, a couple of German-speaking climbers, but as I did not recognise them, I refrained from disturbing them. I went up and down the airfield, talking with the various expeditions and gleaning information about the present condition of the Baltoro Glacier. The news was not encouraging. There was by all accounts lots of snow in the mountains and overpowering heat during the long march in.

When Peter and I had retrieved our luggage, we took a jeep into Skardu. After we had settled in the usual Rest House, Khaled and I walked into town to buy the last bits and pieces we needed. Peter was suffering with a bad headache and stayed behind with the equipment.

We passed a long row of houses and then turned into the dusty lanes where most of the shops were situated. I had prepared a list of all the things we should buy – meal for the chapatis, sugar, dried fruit, and petrol as well as a stove. We hoped to be able to take care of everything here. Although we were strangers, the native Baltis were as friendly and helpful as one finds in tourist resorts the world over. Expeditions pass through this remote district every week, shopping, photographing and wandering the lanes. One result was that the Bazaar, the shopping quarter, was poorly stocked and I began to worry that we wouldn't find all we wanted. The flour and sugar I managed to buy, and later also the dried fruit, but it took several hours to track down a stove. It was a do-it-yourself thing, a petrol cooker, that would serve us during the march-in and at Base Camp. But petrol – that was another matter.

At last I saw a metal sign promising what I sought 'Petrol'. It had been Khaled's idea to try this particular bazaar, a narrow alley with at least a hundred stalls, dusty and hot. A smell of petrol wafted from the rusty tank on the floor. It was late afternoon by this time and the sun was going down, but it was still high enough to shine obliquely over the flat roofs opposite and right into the open petrol booth, and it was as if its slanting rays were stirring up the dust and the smell. Men and children gathered outside as we went into the shop. It was stifling – I wished we could get far away from this place, but we needed to have petrol at all costs.

One of the men in the shop explained that petrol was in short supply and regretted he had none for sale. Khaled tried to explain that we were desperate; without it we couldn't go into the Karakorum; couldn't even go to Dassu, the next village, if there was none for the jeeps. Yes, but . . . yes, but.

They debated long, the men in the shop and the onlookers outside on the narrow street. At last we were allowed our petrol. The precious liquid was measured out with an old tin can, litre by litre, as I waited patiently. Patience is something one learns here – to wait the whole evening if necessary. Normally I find it very difficult to hang about for anything, and do so only with increasing irritation, but here in Skardu, waiting is just another fact of life, like eating or sleeping.

To be on the safe side, I felt we should try out our new cooker. I poured a little of the petrol into its flask-shaped tank, tightened up all its screws, then went out into the street with my strange contraption. It looked far more suited to a medieval alchemist than as an item of equipment for a modern expedition. I pumped it vigorously, lit the

111

burner, and – it worked!

There I squatted in the dusty street with my stove, a babble of excited voices over my head, and all around the naked, grime-encrusted feet of the children. As I looked up, the men in the shop all beamed at me. Our foray into the old bazaar had paid off. We now had petrol and a stove that worked. The expedition could proceed.

We bagan to retrace our steps to the Rest House, pushing a way through the crowds. Basically, I love eastern cities, but I just couldn't get used to Skardu, where there is not a blade of grass to be seen, where the wind unremittingly carries clouds of dust through the streets, and the stench of urine pervades everything. Obviously I had been too spoiled by European cities, and by Rawalpindi even, to feel at home in this remote spot. One needs to have been away on an expedition for a long time before suffering these dirty and poverty-stricken conditions gladly. I could not then foresee how Skardu, on our return march from Hidden Peak, would seem an oasis of comfort to us, a place in which we could buy tea, eat meat, stay in a resthouse with beds and fresh water and be able to wash properly again and rest and eat our fill.

I decided to scout once more round the old and new bazaars just to make sure there was nothing we had forgotten. Quite by chance, on my way back I came upon a poor trader selling dried grapes. As we didn't have much dried fruit, I decided to buy a few kilos from him. But as he was measuring them out with a shovel, I suddenly resolved to purchase the whole sackful. The man was astonished and as delighted as a child. The grapes tasted good, even if they were a bit dusty and mixed with a liberal sprinkling of gravel. "They will bring a touch of variety to our monotonous diet", I thought.

Back at the Rest House, the first porter had already shown up. Khaled had ordered them for that evening, and later on a few more arrived. By 6 o'clock we had twelve, the number we needed for ferrying our 300 kilos of equipment into the Karakorum. I bargained with them for a long time. They were three times as expensive as in Nepal. Naturally, we didn't pay in advance, but we settled the conditions of hire. I promised the standard rate – 40 rupees a day – and double that if they managed two stages in a single day. I made it clear that they must take sufficient food for themselves. As a bonus I promised each man some Atta (ground corn-meal) but up in the mountains they wouldn't be able to find any additional food. I had been told of other parties who had experienced great difficulties because there wasn't enough food for their porters; the men had not catered for themselves and so, after a week, the whole expedition had had to turn back. In order to avoid any similar misadventure, I had bought much more corn-meal than I thought the porters would need. I wanted to be on the safe side.

Each porter would carry about 10 kilogrammes of his own luggage (a blanket, some articles of clothing, flour, butter, some sugar and tea) and 18, or at most 20, kilos of expedition equipment, making a total load of about 30 kilos each. However, I warned them that, barring illness, only those that got their loads to Base Camp would be paid. There would be nothing for shirkers or deserters.

"Anyone who gives up before Base Camp won't get a single rupee; he can go to the devil! Understood?"

"OK" muttered some. "Hunza, hunza", some others.

This bargaining with the porters was a delicate matter. Most of them had been on several expeditions before and knew all the tricks of trying to squeeze money out of us; they knew very well how dependent we were upon them. The men promised to be there early the next morning at 4 o'clock, then they went back to their huts.

Peter and I sat a long time that evening outside the Rest House, looking down at the Braldo River, which had at the same time, the appearance of being both sluggish and stormy. This river flows from the mouth of the Baltoro Glacier and was the line we must follow during the coming days. We had to take the track along it as far as Shigar, then continue along its bank to the last villages. From there we were faced with the endless march over the Baltoro Glacier to Base Camp.

The dirty dust-dry town began to look more friendly as the sun went down. Blue smoke hung over the huts and a last warm glow tinted the highest summits all around. Skardu, lying at around 2,400 metres above sea level, is the principal town in Baltistan; it is surrounded on all sides by high golden-brown mountains, completely bare of any vegetation. Baltistan borders Tibet in the East, India and Kashmir in the south, Gilgit in the west, and the Chinese province of Sinkiang in the north. Known by the name of 'Little Tibet', this former kingdom was for a long time only accessible to explorers and adventurers. For years it has been a mountaineer's paradise, but until now, he has been spared the invasion of ordinary tourism. In this region, contained in quite a narrow area, a number of seven and eight-thousand metre peaks are concentrated, among them K2, which at 8,611 metres is the second highest mountain in the world, and Hidden Peak (known also as Gasherbrum I) which is tucked away at the head of the Baltoro Glacier. Expeditions have been coming into Skardu and Baltistan for 80 years. The inhabitants are therefore quite used to seeing outsiders, and in fact, enjoy a modest prosperity as a result of the mountaineers' visits.

113

After I had posted a letter to Uschi, I returned to the Rest House and went to bed. We needed to be fresh the next morning for the start of our long trek.

When morning did come, we stood and shivered outside the Rest House for three hours waiting for the jeeps to arrive, which had been promised for 4 o'clock. At 5 o'clock the porters arrived, but there was still no sign of the vehicles. The weather was good, a fine bright morning. Women, with children clinging to their knees, peeped round the corner of the nearby huts. Peter and I were raring to be off and cursed this July 13th, which had brought more interminable waiting with it.

Finally at 7 o'clock the jeeps showed up. Their late arrival, they apologised, was on account of the universal petrol shortage. They had spent the whole previous evening and this morning driving around the town trying to collect enough petrol for the journey to Dassu and back. Peter and I put as good a face on it as we could, and loaded up the boxes into the two trucks. We jumped into the first one, Khaled into the second, and the porters divided themselves between the two, packed in tight with all the baggage. Half an hour later the two overloaded vehicles raced through the streets of the town towards the Braldo Bridge, accompanied by swirling clouds of dust. We crossed the bridge and two sand bars and were on the other side of the valley.

Shortly after leaving Skardu, we had our first breakdown. Something had dropped off the second truck, and our vehicle had to go back and look for it. More delay. I noticed that the apricots would soon be ripe and made a mental note to come back to this valley and try them some day.

After repairs, we continued on our dusty way, sometimes at speed, sometimes at a snail's pace. We had a short rest in the village of Shigar, where we drank tea at a Rest House. In the scorching midday heat, we continued up the valley, over rivers and steep passes. We travelled through other villages, lurching along the river bed, until a few miles before Dassu, the road came to an end. Here we unloaded our gear and I paid off the drivers.

Shortly afterwards we began distributing our boxes and sacks among the porters, which was no simple matter as they would squabble amongst themselves for the lightest and most manageable loads. It was quite a while before each porter had his allotted 20 kilogrammes, which he had to see as far as Base Camp.

An hour later our caravan got under way. Peter and I restrained ourselves from dashing off in front. We wanted to stay with the porters to start with, to keep them moving in a single file. This was not easy and soon tried our patience, for the coolies would set down their loads and rest every five or ten minutes. We passed through Dassu, past the last green patches, a few plots beside the river, each no larger than a table-top. That night we camped together under a large boulder beside the turbulent Braldo.

It was still dark when I was awakened the next morning by the sound of the porters preparing breakfast. To the left and right of our campsite, little fires were burning. The sky was dark and overcast, the foaming Braldo rolled its burden of stones along its bed with a noise like thunder. An hour later we were ready to continue. Since Skardu everything had gone well and Peter and I allowed ourselves the hope that we should yet reach Base Camp in good time. The path began to climb steeply and we soon outstripped the porters, intending to wait for them at the head of the pass. But as Khaled was with them, we pressed on further, along a straight stretch and towards 9 o'clock in the morning we reached Chakpo, a fertile oasis where a tributary of the Braldo came in from the right.

After a week of 'expedition bureaucracy', when one eventually leaves it all behind, it is like a holiday after weeks of hard work. One suddenly has time to meditate and take stock. I am firmly convinced that many overworked businessmen would not find it a waste of time to take part in an expedition like this. These long marches, day after day, are the surest, if not the only, way to avoid spiritual blindness. They provide the possibility, or rather the necessity, of uniting the active and contemplative components of one's nature. This is never more easily achieved than on a long trek through lonely mountain valleys.

Life for the inhabitants of Chakpo is simple and hard. We had been resting on one of their flat terraced roofs and trying to obtain eggs, chapatis and lassi (curdled milk), also some tea to quench our thirst. Women with long colourful dresses squatted in front of their shanty-like dwellings, which were piled one on top of the other. They disappeared, however, as soon as one turned one's gaze towards them. The tiny huts were dark; their walls of loose stones cemented together with mud, were crumbling; their little windows, no bigger than one's head, were screened with wooden trellis-work.

We wanted to erect our camp on a rough meadow at the edge of the village. We asked a native farmer if this would be permitted. He nodded and we settled down to await the arrival of our porters. We had only been there half an hour when some villagers came up, bringing chickens that they hoped to barter with us. But they were too expensive and we only bought a little flour for the porters, to eke out our existing stocks.

As on the previous nights, it looked like rain, and the porters soon found themselves shelter in a nearby stable. They promised to be ready in good time the next morning. It rained all night and there was no sign of any let-up in the morning. The porters had all stolen off into the nearby huts and we had a job rounding them up and trying to persuade them to move. The path would be much more dangerous in the wet, they objected. It was not until about 8 o'clock that the first of them emerged, but two were still missing. We waited half an hour. . . an hour . . . and still they did not turn up. At last we tracked them down in a narrow cave-like hovel, where they were playing dice with the locals. They were very surprised to see me come in, and it was only after I shouted at them, that they left their game and followed me outside.

"If you don't want to carry on", I said "you can leave the expedition here and now. Go back home – but you don't get paid."

At that, they followed me back to the campsite and we could at last get on our way. It was already late in the morning.

In the sultry midday we made good going, if a little slow. To the left and right of our path the valley sides reared up steeply. The rain had stopped for an hour or two, and the sun's rays, shining through the rising mists, seemed to be magnified as through a burning glass. There was an ever-present menace of stonefalls and it was difficult to decide the safest way to proceed through this ravine.

A light drizzle was falling again and I was in the middle of the column, when suddenly, some porters came running back waving their arms. Their faces were marked with terror as they charged past me and down to where the valley widened out. I was quite unable to stop them. It was only when I reached the place from where they had turned back, that I saw what had alarmed them. What in the dry season is a harmless side-stream had become a foaming torrent, hurling down mud and boulders as big as baggage trunks. Ten metres lower down it gushed into the Braldo River, which swallowed up all the stones and sediment without even changing colour. This was, as it appeared, a singularly hazardous place to attempt a crossing. The porters had recognised right away that we wouldn't get over as long as the rain lasted.

On the brink of the boiling river, Peter and I discussed our situation. The porters had already begun lighting little fires and huddling under the rocks, brewing up some tea. Some of them had found a little cave and were preparing to settle themselves in for the night. Repeatedly I tried to get them to move on. I said we would find a safer spot higher up and span the river with a fixed rope. We would take their loads across for them.

"You'll only have to get yourselves across", I cajoled. But they resisted.

116

"Further on", they protested, "are some very dangerous slopes. We could not cross them now; there will be too much danger from stonefalls."

"We will make them safe for you!"

Still they refused. Nothing would make them budge an inch so long as it rained, not even the promise of extra money.

Peter and I were in despair. Another day lost. However, it was still early afternoon and we could not give up so easily. We resolved to go a bit further and spy out the land. We were hoping to find a shallower crossing that would not present the same difficulties. Whilst I belayed him on a rope, Peter climbed down the vertical wall of mud, as high as a house, into the murky, stone-filled water. He gingerly stretched a foot out to the first stepping stone, thus straddled, he then ventured to take the next decisive step; finally he waded, up to his knees in slime, across to the opposite bank, and swarmed up the steep slope.

We anchored the rope to rocks on both banks, then I followed across on the fixed rope, and we hurried, sometimes scrambling, sometimes running, along the extraordinarily awkward and dangerous river bank, as far as the first heap of moraine that barred the view ahead. There seemed to be no end to this precarious traverse, with its continual threat of falling stones. The track, barely wider than a foot, had for the most part been washed away. The only possible route ran so close to the Braldo that our feet were bathed in its spray. It was scarcely possible to keep one's footing on these slimy slopes, and a single fall would be enough to plunge us into the Braldo's flood. There would be no chance of survival. And all the time, the stones kept falling, threatening to strike us down.

After an hour, we too were convinced that the porters were right. It was out of the question to bring a column of fifteen men across these slopes. So we had no alternative but to return to the porters and sit it out.

CLOSE TO DEFEAT

There was no sign of a break in the rain that afternoon, so we decided to bivouac there and then. If it improved the next day we would go on. The porters in the meantime had discovered a second cave and were settling themselves well in. Peter and I pitched our tent under some overhanging rocks and did our best to sleep, cramped closely together as we were. Our hopes for better weather were dashed in the evening, when it began to rain even harder, drumming on the tent roof. Even the acrid smoke, listlessly curling out of the porters' caves seemed to portend bad weather. Hours of despondency followed, hours during which we had to admit that success hung in the balance, more so than on earlier undertakings.

"We're lost" Peter began to voice his fears, "if we have to hang about here for a couple of days. We might as well go straight home now."

"It's bound to clear up, sooner or later it has to get better."

"For as long as those slopes ahead of us remain wet, we'll never get the porters to take another step. They know just how dangerous that steep scree is, and they're quite right not to want to go on."

"It will stay dangerous all the time the ground is wet, but if the sun were to dry it out a bit, the stones would stop coming down and we'd get the porters through OK. You'll see. Perhaps tomorrow even."

"I don't see any sign of a change tomorrow."

"I must confess, nor do I. If we have to wait too long, it will be too late."

Immersed in our thoughts, we lay there. I now began to think that we had been foolish to set off on such a venture. Back home I had thought our chances good, it seemed we really could have pulled off my dream of a two-man ascent of an eight-thousander. Now, condemned to idleness, it didn't look as if we would ever get any further than this. We might just as well have stayed at home. Caught in this unhappy situation, our prospects for the rest of the trek looked very gloomy indeed. We were only at the beginning and the most difficult stages still lay ahead when we reached the mighty Baltoro Glacier. We had at least two more weeks of approach march in front of us. I hadn't yet reached that stage of humble resignation to fate, which sometimes comes after months of effort towards a single objective. I couldn't sleep for worrying about the future of the expedition. Our despair intensified with the incessant rain and we began to feel trapped in a situation beyond our control. We discussed for hours the possibility of abandoning our project. We might yet beat a retreat and turn our attention to another mountain, Nanga Parbat perhaps, which could be reached in a few days, or some peak in the Eastern Hindu Kush.

As it was still raining the next morning, we outlined the situation to Khaled and asked him what he thought we should do. He did not know what to say. I asked him if it would be politically possible to go to Nanga Parbat instead, and when he said yes, it would, we were in a bigger quandary than ever, chewing over the various possibilities and our own inclinations.

Towards 9 o'clock, after the rain had been stopped for about an hour, the porters suddenly decided to go on. Peter and I were so surprised at this turn of events, we immediately forgot all our indecision. We didn't hesitate for a moment, and handled the men with kid gloves for fear they would again change their minds. With the rope fixed over the raging torrent, we brought the whole troop over, one by one, securing each man to the rope with a running karabiner. With Peter in the lead and myself in the middle of the column, we continued our way up the valley. The side of the gorge towering over us was more dangerous than the North Wall of the Eiger. At intervals we would all stand still and scan the treacherous scree slopes, which rose for 400 metres over our heads. Only when all seemed quiet would we dash on to the next spot that promised a measure of safety. As one ran forward, next man carefully watched for possible signs of danger. A slip here would almost certainly plunge one into the swollen river. The Braldo is between 60 and 80 metres wide at this spot and no man would stand a chance if he fell in. The waters were trundling down boulders as large as dining tables, and their roar drowned out all other sounds.

There seemed to be no end to this hazardous traverse. Whilst Peter hurried on ahead to reconnoitre the way, I stayed with the porters, holding them back till he gave us the nod to join him.

This was the only technique possible to evade the stonefalls. Suddenly, in the middle of a particularly steep and narrow section, the slope above us came alive. Peter was right in the middle of the line of fire as the first salvos whirred down.

"Stonefall!"

Nimble as a cat, he dodged the stones and took refuge under an overhanging boulder, the next sheltered spot. One porter who had been right behind him, came back shouting and gesticulating to the others that they should not go a step further. I quickly sized up the

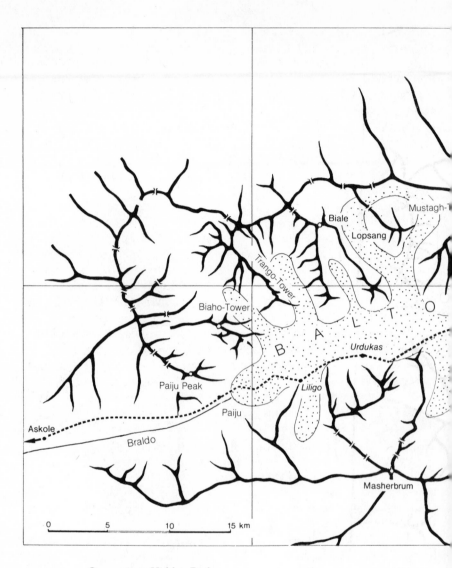

Map labels: Mustagh-, Biale, Lopsang, Trango-Tower, Biaho-Tower, B A L T O, Paiju Peak, Urdukas, Liligo, Paiju, Askole, Braldo, Masherbrum

0   5   10   15 km

••••••• = Our route to Hidden Peak.

situation. I knew it would cost us several more days if we gave up now and retreated with our porters to a safe place lower down. As soon as I was sure no more stones were on their way down, I grasped the lead porter by the wrist and marched him the full length of the gully. Once through this stone-spitting ravine, he had no wish to retrace his steps and tempt fate again. For the others, there was nothing left to do, but follow. With great caution and at a signal from us, they came one after

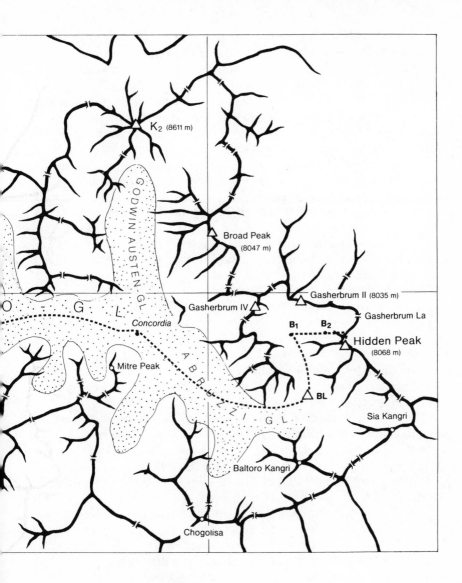

K₂ (8611 m)

GODWIN AUSTEN GL.

Broad Peak
(8047 m)

Gasherbrum II (8035 m)

Gasherbrum IV

Gasherbrum La

O   G.   L.

B₁   B₂

Concordia

Hidden Peak
(8068 m)

A B R U Z Z I · GL.

Mitre Peak

BL

Sia Kangri

Baltoro Kangri

Chogolisa

the other safely through. So far, so good.

It took all our concentration and skill and another two hours to traverse the rest of this section. We were at such a heightened pitch of awareness, ready for instant reaction, that it seemed we heard sounds not just with our ears, but with our whole bodies. If something began falling down, if danger threatened, we knew it before our standard senses became aware of it. By the time we reached the end of this first scree slope, several kilometres long, we were almost played out, but immediately commenced the passage of a second, shorter one.

Just then I saw four men coming down towards us. I was astonished to recognise the celebrated Joe Brown, Leader of the British Trango Tower Expedition. With him were Ian McNaught Davis, Giulio Fiocchi – leader of an Italian Expedition to the Grand Cathedral – and a young Italian. Joe Brown was obviously dead beat. He slumped down beside us on the scree. Small of build, and no longer young, he looked all played out with his greying hair and his face slightly swollen. His eyes were heavy and glazed, the strain and effort of the march down from Trango, were easily read in his features. I had always admired this man, the first to climb Mustagh Tower and Kangchenjunga, and I knew how tough he was, so it was easy to imagine what lay in store for us. Brown was amazed to learn what we were proposing to do, and just said fatalistically "Well, have a look at it anyway." His hard years now lay behind him.

Peter and I chatted briefly with the four and learned how they had fared. The British had been unlucky, but the Italians had two successes to their credit. As our porters had now caught up with us, we continued on our way. We were very relieved to see the back of these infernal scree slopes and laboriously struggled up the steep rise on the right of the river (our right, the river's true left bank). Peter and I hurried on ahead and had soon lost sight of the porters. I was having a job to keep up with Peter and stopped to look around for a possible campsite, without success. We were plagued by hunger and thirst. A piece of chapati, or a couple of potatoes would have been enough, but there was no prospect of finding anything before we reached the next village. During the march-in, we lived entirely 'off the land', refraining from eating any of our stock of tins or cheese on these stretches between villages.

As we reached the top of the rise, we looked back at the seemingly-endless, narrow grey-brown gorge. So that's that done, we thought. The Braldo was now 500 metres below us, but its roar could still plainly be heard. Far ahead, at the next bend in the valley, a few trees were visible. Probably this was Chongo, the next settlement.

"The porters will soon catch us up. Khaled is with them; let's go on", I urged.

Hours later we began to wonder if we were still on the right track. There wasn't a tree or bush to offer any shade, no overhanging rocks. I went ahead up a steep, precipitous path which then wound down again, the other side. Once I found a cigarette packet on the stones; so we weren't the first Europeans to pass this way. Silently, Peter and I marched on, one behind the other.

THE LAST VILLAGES

We had studied the map in the morning before setting off, but it had not seemed that the way would be so long. Perhaps the porters would have slowed down in the midday heat. Could they still reach Chongo before nightfall?

Under a rugged rock buttress, we finally saw the village, just a few jumbled huts and terraced fields between the river and the grim cliff. This small green stretch of land, bounded upriver by a rock spur, jutting into the Braldo, downstream by a lateral valley, was three kilometres long and 500 metres wide. Room for fields and huts for twenty families. But each year two or three more came. Sometimes six or eight people lived together in the narrowest space. And each year the land available for cultivation diminished. The Braldo nibbled it away at the bottom, whilst the rockfalls buried it by the acre, at the top of the village. The land and the villagers were constantly threatened. The place seemed so dangerous to me that I wouldn't even have contemplated putting a Base Camp there.

We climbed a pair of rickety ladders onto the roof of a house. It was the front yard of the hut above. No-one was about. Only a few hens scratching and a dilapidated bedstead with a few covers on it, upon which we sat. There was a sharp wind blowing up here. After we had sat awhile, I called out, but nobody came. The women were all in the fields, the boys and men obviously off with some expedition or other. Whilst we sat there patiently, we wondered what the local people would be like.

I looked across the rooftops and tried to imagine what life must be like up here – hostile, monotonous, hard, if we apply our standards to it. The pale mud roofs shone now in the sun. When I looked from the green fields back to these mud buildings, my eyes hurt, so dazzling was the glare.

After a while, an old man came out onto the terrace. He stood a little way from us, and Peter and I greeted him.

"Salam!"

He returned the greeting and came nearer. Peter held out his right

123

hand. The old man took it and pressed it between his own horny palms, gently, almost stroking it, as if weighing its weight against his own. When he had finished his greeting ceremony, he tapped Peter on the shoulder. I said no, for I understood his question, and we began to converse with each other in sign language. I told him that we did not need any more porters, that ours would soon be here. The weathered face of the old man tightened.

"Sahib?" he asked, pointing to Peter and then to me.

I indicated with two outstretched fingers that there were just the two of us, only two Sahibs. But also twelve coolies and a Captain. With my hands and a few words of Balti that I had picked up, I explained it to him. He wanted to know where the coolies came from and where we were going. At the name 'Gasherbrum' his eyes twinkled. He gave us to understand that he had been there as a porter himself.

Shortly afterwards a young boy brought up some eggs, and another, some tea and chapatis. It was late afternoon by this time. The villagers came home from the fields – women with baskets full of grass, and children running behind, a man with a hoe, young girls giggling. Somewhere music played from a transistor radio.

The sinking sun caught the grass and the wind freshened. Golden haze filled the V-shaped notch of the valley. Far to the west dark bands of cloud masked the horizon. Only above us did the sun continue to shine.

We were still sitting on the roof when the porters arrived. They found quarters in a stall, and this time we stayed with them.

When we went for a short stroll that evening, we met Martin Boysen, the lead-climber of the British Trango Tower team. He told us that their expedition had got off to a good start, but on the final assault, 200 metres from the top, his knee had become inextricably wedged in a narrow crack. He was left hanging, unable to move an inch up or down. His companion had gone down for bivouac equipment and food, but Martin did not want to wait so long for help. In desperation he hacked away at the fabric of his trousers with a piton and eventually freed himself. Then he roped down the mountain and the attempt was over.

We also spoke of the Everest Expedition planned for the autumn of 1975 with Chris Bonington in the lead, and wished Martin all luck on his next enterprise.

From Chongo we went on to Askole the next morning, two hours distant. The way led past villages and through green fields. The landscape which till now had been drear and desolate, began to resemble valleys in the Western Alps. Far away Mango Gusar raised its sharp white head, and to the right rose some five-thousander peaks. The sumptuous green of the irrigated fields contrasted sharply with the arid slopes between the valley floor and the snowy summits.

Peter and I still hoped to get further that day, but the porters made it clear they felt they had earned a rest day. As Askole was the last village, we told them to buy boots and food. Meanwhile we contacted the 'Lambadar', the Mayor. We purchased some flour and butter, and a sheep for the porters. We would have liked to buy another as well, but there were hardly any sheep in the village itself and the farms were too high above in the side valleys for one to be fetched quickly.

We set up our tents on a small, muddy patch on the side of the village nearest the mountains. Some of the inhabitants came up and we tried to hire some extra porters from amongst them, but it proved impossible because the most suitable men were already away with the American K2 Expedition or the Italian Baltoro Expedition. In the afternoon we wandered through the village. Women were carting manure to the fields, men were squatting on the roofs of their houses and would greet us from a long way off "Salem Aleikum!"

The whole of that evening we sat in front of our tent and chatted with the locals about earlier expeditions. I was delighted that some of them should recall the fifties so clearly; in particular there were some men who had accompanied the Italian K2 Expedition twenty years before, and still remembered it in detail. Riccardo Cassin, our Old Man from Lhotse, was well-known here, but I noticed from allusions and anecdotes that it was Walter Bonatti who was held in the greatest respect. Bonatti had been to K2 in 1954 and was regarded as the strong man of that party; later he came back and climbed Gasherbrum IV, a glittering pyramid in the furthest recess of the Baltoro. They told how on the march-in, he had climbed a completely smooth boulder near Urdukas, by a single fist-sized crack.

We left Askole on the morning of July 18th. We hoped to do a double stage that day and reach the bridge beyond Korofon. There was a lot of activity around the houses and on the track as our loaded column moved out of the village. The air was cool as we made our way through the last fields to a narrow gorge at the end of the valley. Some women in their traditional dark clothes, were stooping in the knee-high corn, weeding. Others were busy driving the cows to the stony upper pastures.

Although we were by no means the first expedition to cross the Biafo Glacier this year, we still had considerable difficulty finding the route and piloting the porters across it. This dead glacier changes day by day, and the tracks of other expeditions disappear in a few days. In spite of a few difficulties on the glacier and the broiling sun, we reached Joila in the afternoon, where in summer a suspension bridge crossing a tributary of the Braldo, offers the only possible way ahead.

We chose the left bank of the river as our campsite. James Whittaker and his American K2 team were already installed there on their way home after an unsuccessful attempt on the world's second highest mountain. They kept popping over to pass the time of day with us. The Italian expedition, whose leader Fiocchi we had met a few days ago, was camped on the other bank of the river. I knew some of the young Italians well and we found a lot to talk about. They passed on some useful tips for the days ahead, and somehow their success had the effect of strengthening our own morale.

From the Americans we learned that they had seen the Schell party and were of the opinion that they too were heading for Hidden Peak. We were not at all happy about this news: it was we who had the permit for Hidden Peak and although we had been in touch with Schell, nothing had been agreed between us. Moreover, no-one from their group had waited for us in Rawalpindi, so we no longer felt able to agree that the two expeditions be united.

Peter and I therefore decided to separate. We wanted to catch up with Schell and stop him in good time so that his party could still go for the peak which the Government had allotted to them. The longer they stayed on Hidden Peak, even on the ordinary route, they would be wasting energy and material and time. Peter would therefore go on ahead the next day and reach Base Camp in three or four days. Having had more experience with porters, I undertook to see them and the equipment into Base Camp.

On the spur of the moment the Italians invited us to supper. Peter decided to stay behind as he would have to start before dawn the next morning and wanted to sleep. Night was falling as I balanced my way across the swaying wickerwork bridge to the Italian camp on the other side of the river. The minestrone may have been a bit too salty, but the general atmosphere was warm and gay. We talked long and animatedly. As Peter and I were somewhat short on food and didn't know exactly how long we would have to stay in Base Camp, I asked the Italians if they had any to spare, a little something for the march-in perhaps, even enough for one day would be a help. But they refused as they still had their own return march to the first villages, and then another week on to Skardu. They were not sure they would have enough for themselves, but assured me they had left a quantity of bread and tinstuffs at their Base Camp.

"The porters will have had those already", I laughed.

"Yes, you're probably right. They don't usually leave anything, not even an empty can."

As I said goodbye and handed the deputy leader a letter for Uschi, that I had written stage by stage over the last three days, one of the group, Giorgio Panzeri, took me to one side. He pushed a nylon bag into my hand with all sorts of goodies inside. "Some titbits for your march-in" he said. There was chocolate and dried fruit that he had obviously been saving for his own return journey, and a little card with the words "Un sacco di auguri – Giorgio", a bag full of blessings. I was very touched and surprised by the generosity of this young Italian, who knew that his older comrades were not prepared to underwrite our mini-expedition – after all, they reasoned, it was we who had deliberately limited ourselves to 200 kgs. of luggage, so we must take the consequences.

Giorgio is one of the best Italian climbers. Only just twenty years old, he had already done all the most important routes in the Alps and had an impressive number of solo ascents to his credit also. He had twice been awarded the 'Griguetta d'oro', an annual climbing prize for a climber under 24 who has distinguished himself in the Alps.

ON FOOT TO NIRVANA

There is a kind of loneliness to which one never gets accustomed. That is the isolation of facing danger alone. It was already after 10 o'clock when I left the Italian camp. A July night, one of those clear Karakorum nights that we were later to experience often. The moon was hidden somewhere behind the mountains and yet it was still bright as I approached the rickety bridge; I could even see the water shimmering below. The black strands, of which the bridge was fashioned, were scarcely visible and it took a great effort to negotiate them in the dark. I clung tightly to the coarse open ropes, as thick as young tree trunks. The nearer I came to the middle of the river, the more solitary I felt, and the more keenly I wished I had stayed the night with the Italians. I could plainly see the foaming water, its waves and eddies, between the three strands of the walkway. I had to be so careful not to succumb to the lure of the waters, liquid silver in the starlight, not to lose my balance. The suspension bridge swayed with my steps. I was quite giddy by the time I reached the other side and clambered up the steep bank. I had crossed to another world, with the bridge as the last link with humanity, behind me. On my way to my tent I thought again that in a few hours Peter wanted to be on his way, and I should be left alone with the responsibility for getting the Liaison Officer and the twelve porters to Base Camp without incident.

I had drunk my morning tea before the sun's first rays fanned out behind the horn of Mango Gusar. My gloomy apprehensions had fled with the morning light. I was even glad now at the prospect of being on my own. As we struck camp, I saw a faint glimmer of enthusiasm flicker across the faces of the porters and knew that they would go well and that we should make good progress in the days ahead.

I hurried out in front to explore the route and to be able to travel at my own pace. On the left of the river, I slowed down a bit and soon came to a level patch of moraine on which some scrubby plants and yellowish clumps of grass were growing. I looked for a spring, and finding none, went down to the nearby river and washed myself in its olive-green glacier water. I had now forgotten the troublesome,

128

unpleasant experiences of the first few days of the approach march, and here on the brink of the Braldo, I experienced a deep inner calm. Later, as I was walking again through the mountains, it burst over me anew. I felt happy, confident and free of all complications. The savage peaks around me had awoken my courage and taste for freedom. There was no need for words but I was anxious to get going and quickened my steps, which were accompanied by the continuous rustle of dry grass. I ought really to have waited for the others, but the warm morning sun, the river rushing by and my curiosity, would not permit me to dally. I was happy to be walking on my own. I had got into the habit of speaking my thoughts half aloud. Without taking the trouble to formulate them exactly or to follow them through logically, I would say a few words, then my mind would flit to something else so that the train of thought was broken and I would be off on a different tack.

Leaving the moraine where my feet just wallowed in the loose sand, I climbed up some scree that had collected between the river and the steep slope above. By degrees I drew nearer to a solitary plant, growing ahead. Although it was a poor specimen with few leaves, it seemed a horticultural treasure to me. All around was perfect peace. It is true the river thundered to my right and flies buzzed around my head, but these sounds failed to disturb the general harmony, nor did the distant singing of the wind on the ridges and summits. Every now and then I would hear the voices of our porters – even these toned in with the solitude. As I stood waiting for them to appear, my eyes followed a little cloud which had built up over the summit of Mango Gusar. Only when the file of coolies appeared in the distance, did I slowly continue my way.

I was right, I thought, to take advantage of the permit. If it had just been a snap decision, a sudden flash of enthusiasm like a straw fire – this challenge of two men against an eight-thousander – I would not have been standing here now. We would have given up days ago at the Braldo Traverse. But we hadn't. I was now convinced that our enterprise stood a good chance of success.

As Peter crossed the dead glacier completely alone, he automatically considered the possibility of returning to Paiju, where he knew I would be camping with the main party. But he didn't turn back. He marched resolutely onwards, keeping well in mind the real object of his haste – to get to the Base Camp of the Schell party and stop them climbing Hidden Peak. It was already growing dark as he prepared to camp at Liligo. There were no more clouds in the west. They had retreated behind Paiju Peak and the sky was full of stars. He listened to

129

the rattling of the stones falling off the edge of the moraine into the crevasses. He kept gazing up at the Milky Way, seemingly so close, diagonally spanning the immense valley in which he bivouaced.

Peter had a headache, which usually happened when he gained altitude too quickly, but he took nothing for it and just put up with it.

"We'll do it", he thought, as he lay there trying to sleep.

This new feeling of being completely alone worried him less than the tedious march with the porters, the continual uncertainty, and the worry of looking after them. But as he would not be seeing them for some days, he had fresh worries. Suppose they got held up somewhere, or did not make fast enough progress.

What a marvellous thing it is to be young! This euphoric observation came to me as I clambered up and down the little hills of moraine and could see, far away in the distance, the terminal moraine at the snout of the Baltoro Glacier. To the left and right stood massive granite towers and far away in the dark ranges, somewhere lay K2. I sat down to rest under a boulder, sheltered from the vertical rays of the sun. I wanted to wait for the porters and take a good look at my surroundings, which, each day we moved forward, became more and more exciting.

Meanwhile it had now become afternoon, a hot, dry, sultry afternoon. It was out of the question to rest in the direct sun. The rocks shimmered in the hot haze, the sand and rocks seemed to glow. Yet the sky was gradually clouding over. A breath of wind sprang up, blowing little clouds of dust off the glacier. For a short while even the glowing ball of the sun was hidden behind the accumulating mass of cirrus cloud, and two hours later it at least became pleasantly cool. In another half an hour the sun broke through again, and I stood up, greedily inhaling the fresh air. I climbed down to the Braldo and had a thorough top-to-toe wash. It was like a tingling cold shower. I felt an urge to go on, simply to see what lay around the next corner; I didn't want to wait for the porters any longer but to forget the expedition for a couple of hours more. But though I was sorely tempted, I had to stay where I was. I knew the porters would not reach Paiju if I was not there to encourage them on. From there we would be able to start up the Baltoro Glacier the next day. So I sat down again under my overhanging boulder and went to sleep.

I didn't wake up until 5 o'clock in the afternoon, feeling jaded and sleepy. I had a headache and was overcome with dizziness as I tried to stand up. I looked around but could not see anyone. Then lower down, I heard the noise of stones rolling into the river. Going back a bit, I could see the porters trying to cross a side-stream of the Braldo and having trouble keeping their footing in the bubbling coffee-brown water. In the few hours since I had crossed it, the stream had swollen into a dangerous torrent. I ran back and tried to help as best I could, leaning across from my side of the stream with a long stick. When they had all come across, I made it clear that we must go on for another hour till we got to Paiju, where there was fresh water and firewood.

Paiju is the local name for the campsite directly beneath the unclimbed six-thousander of the same name, about half an hour before the snout of the Baltoro Glacier. This Paiju camp is beautifully situated with a fine view; its two springs give only a trickle of water, but always such fresh, clear water, a rarity in this wilderness landscape. However, the whole campsite was liberally covered in the ordure from previous expeditions, and I had extreme difficulty in finding a more or less clean spot where I could camp. As the sky was now clear, I decided to dispense with a tent and sleep under a few trees, whose leaves were constantly quivering in the wind. I spread out some grass upon which to put my sleeping mat and bag. Khaled seemed dead beat, as he had been trundling along at the back of the group all day. He did not even have enough strength to put up his own tent, and I asked the porters to do it for him.

As soon as the Baltis were there and unloaded, a couple of them disappeared up trees and others into holes in the ground. They fetched dry sticks and water and before long set about cooking tea and chapatis in the caves left by other expeditions. Again they had managed a double stage that day and as promised, I paid them the bonus. They were well pleased and brought me some Dhal (lentils) and tea. My hope that we could reach Base Camp in a week or ten days at the most, looked more probable.

I sat in Paiju and pondered again why I was here and why this particular project was so important to me, as I so often did when I was alone in the evenings. They were questions I could not honestly answer, and in the end I resolved just to accept the fact that I was here, so far from home, as being the most natural thing in the world. This was easy to do when I was busy and had no time for such musings. The last few hours when I had been walking alone through the wild landscape, or actively taking responsibility for the progress of the expedition, had been great fun. Handling porters, settling their little differences, finding campsites, sharing out loads each morning – these were all simple, but essential activities to ensure the progress of the expedition. I busied myself with them, not with any missionary zeal, nor for purely mountaineering ends, but because I wanted to fulfil properly the tasks I had set myself. Of course the fact that I was here at all was due, in good measure, to personal ambition. For three years I had dreamt hopefully of climbing my third eight-thousander. But now, on the march in, the prospect of a third height record or a 2-man eight-thousander success, were less important to me than coping with the day to day tasks, as they arose. From my earliest days I had worked towards achieving what is best in climbing and best in human nature, this had been in my mind during my first big tours and expeditions, but now all I wanted was to live without causing trouble to other people.

During my journeys amongst the poorest mountain folk in the world, I have been forced to the belief that it is not really possible to help them, without at the same time doing them harm. It is an illusion to suppose that the world can be improved. Humankind in its entirety is so complex, so diverse, that any attempt to work for its general good is bound to founder against its many contradictions. It may be an interesting exercise to consider such possibilities, but they can never be effected. I am now less and less inclined to place an expedition, or myself, simply in the service of the common good. On the contrary, I have come to the conclusion that a well-balanced life, a life at peace with oneself, is the ultimate ideal. Today I go on expeditions simply for myself, because I want to, and although few people can understand this, I feel these expeditions to be necessary, that is, necessary for me to survive as a human being, to realise myself and maintain an inner harmony.

I enjoy the countryside, but at the same time I take seriously my obligations to look after the needs of the porters and liaison officer, as well as taking care of myself.

The thought which repeatedly tormented me on the long daily marches was how Uschi was faring. What was she doing and thinking? As things were at the moment, I could have brought her along. She was quite competent on account of her expedition experiences, to cope with the trek to Base Camp. But it was possible that she might have become a handicap somewhere along the line, and perhaps later on, she would have been unable to bear the solitude in Base Camp. But was she not abandoned to solitude now? Abandoned through my own naked ambition and completely in the dark as to the outcome of the undertaking?

Eagerly conscientious throughout the day, Khaled would still make his rounds of the porters in the evening. They would all sit around the fires in little groups, making chapatis and cooking them in melted butter. Khaled spoke with them, gesturing expressively with his long slim hands. I gathered from the conversation that he was cheering them up in preparation for the next difficult stage.

One old porter was already curled up, trying to sleep wrapped in an old blanket by the fire, his breathing loud and heavy. Would he make the 70 kilometres to Base Camp? 70 kilometres of glacier with 30 kilos on his back, sleeping in the open at night and with scarcely anything to eat? I gave him a piece of chocolate, which he accepted gratefully.

Back at his sleeping place, Khaled rummaged in his rucksack for his pocket torch, tied it to a branch over his head, took another swig from the flask he kept by the pullover which served as his pillow, and lay down, hoping to forget everything and get to sleep. But to start with, he had difficulty in dropping off, hindered not only by his leaden tiredness, but disturbed by the porters and the constant flickering of the fire. Even later, when the Baltis had all settled down, he found himself still unable to sleep; he listened to the roar of the Braldo and gazed up at the moon, which had risen behind a ragged curtain of cloud.

As I was just about to lie down too, I had the instinctive feeling that someone was there, someone else was coming. I looked round in the direction of the Baltoro Glacier and saw in the pale moonlight, a figure approaching. It was a woman, obviously a climber going home alone. As she approached I fancied I recognised her, but I asked her name all the same. It was Simone Badier, one of the best European lady climbers, who had been with Frehel's French party to Paiju Peak. They had been unsuccessful and Simone, tired and fed up with all the load-carrying, had separated from the rest of the party. She had made a solitary excursion to Urdukas, and on the way back had almost drowned in a glacier stream. Now she was going home and that afternoon had again fallen in a river. She was pleased when I offered her some food and a place to sleep.

We sat there together a long time and I made some tea. The leaves rustled in the trees and the moon glimmered through the network of branches. Then Simone spread out her bed close to mine and we talked until late into the night of all the other expeditions that were in the Baltoro area. For hours I tried to get to sleep without success. Lying in my bag and looking resolutely up through the treetops, I followed the path of the moon.

I woke next morning at 5 o'clock, feeling refreshed and cheered despite the almost sleepless night. I stood up, rummaged for a pen and paper in my rucksack and began to write a letter to Uschi. "I'll give it to Simone to take", I said half-aloud, yielding once more to the habit of solitude. Involuntarily, I then began to think how long it might be before Uschi read this letter in Villnöss. And it brought home to me more than ever before, how far apart we actually were. It could be months before I was with her again; one thing I had not taken into account in any of my calculations, was the uncertain air service between Skardu and Rawalpindi. Simone Badier stuffed the letter into her rucksack and we parted. As she made her way down the valley, I watched for a long time.

The sky over the Baltoro Glacier threatened rain. A few bright patches broke through the heavy clouds and for a moment, the sunrise cast a vermilion glow over the drab steel-grey clouds. Sombre stood the mountains all round, and grey the glacier; not a glimmer of the young day caught its surface.

In rather less than an hour, we reached the terminal moraine. A mighty river issued from the snout of the glacier, and gushed into the wide riverbed of the Braldo. For the porters, the climb up the debris-strewn ice cliff onto the glacier was not only strenuous but also very awkward. Stones kept rolling away under their bare feet, and every now and then, one of them would fall over. Everywhere was the same monotonous scene – debris, water, snow. The Baltoro Glacier was a churned-up sea of ice and detritus, through which we must struggle the 70 kilometres to Base Camp.

I tried to find a more or less negotiable route for the porters, and had to keep waiting for them whilst they rested. Only along the spine of a long moraine, where they could see me a good way off, could I get out in front for a while. Then, when the way led downwards again, I had to stop. New peaks, new valleys. It was like watching a continuous film strip, the same landscape kept repeating itself over and over. Was this really the first time I had passed this spot, or had I already done it once before? This strange feeling of déjà-vu did not leave me all the time I was on the glacier.

Now I saw the porters toiling up onto the back of the moraine and felt the old restlessness to forge ahead. All this standing about was not my scene, but there was usually no choice. Always when the porters were the merest coloured specks in the distance, I would have to stop and wait for them – a stranger in the wilderness, nothing but rock debris and to the left and right of the glacier, rock walls, and above them, the sky.

Each day, often each hour, the sky changed its colour. In early morning, the darkness gave way to violet and sometimes wine red. Now, in the daytime, it was a bright, silky blue with tatters of cloud sailing away over the summits. Like the sky, the glacier too changed its colour. In the first early morning light it was a wet black river of shattered rocks, later becoming, if the morning was fine, a living sculptured surface, full of fine detail. In the mid-day's glare, it glittered amongst its brown stones, fading in the afternoon, till in the evening its rocks were thrown into sharp, monochromatic relief, metallically shiny.

Up till now we had hardly touched our food stores, and we also saved as much fuel as we could for Base Camp. Since Paiju I had not had a hot meal. In the morning a mug of tea from the porter's billie and a piece of bread. In the evening, I allowed myself another piece of bread and a tin of something.

We camped in Liligo. It smelt like a public lavatory, and I was annoyed that I had not been able to bring the porters any further. But the next camp at Urdukas was a full day's march away, and there was, seemingly, nowhere before then.

The next afternoon in Urdukas, I met the Swiss from Sia Kangri. There was a spring and dry ground, and above all, caves for the porters. This was a good place to stop. The campsite, on grass terraces between house-high rocks on the lefthand side of the valley, afforded a singularly fine view of the granite giants opposite – Biaho Tower, Little Cathedral Peak, Trango Towers, Grand Cathedral, Lobsang. Their walls, for the most part vertical, rose for more than 2,000 metres sheer out of the glacier, higher than the highest faces in the Alps.

Next morning it took longer than usual to get the porters going; obviously they were loath to leave the dry ground for the inhospitable, cold, stony glacier. Sometimes one could make out a kind of path in the rubble, not always clearly, but for a stretch the stones might seem to lie flatter than those around. As the Sahib, I went first, although in fact I knew less about the glacier than the porters. Khaled brought up the rear: he had promised as we left Urdukas that morning, to stay at the back all the time. We couldn't be far from the middle of the glacier; the other side of the valley was a gentle basin of green, like a breath of fresh air. As I walked along, I would look into the view-finder of my camera without knowing exactly what I wanted to photograph. At times the view seemed very familiar. Perhaps I recognised it from pictures; certainly not all the mountains were unknown to me.

I had told the porters that they could leave it to me to find the easiest route and they appeared to trust me. I frequently had to stop to get my bearings. It was windy now, a fine dust hung in the air and amongst the dark stones, it was impossible to distinguish any that were lighter in colour than the rest. Had the wind blown all the tracks away? No, wasn't that them again? Like a memory it would suddenly flash to me which way to go, I would seem to see the track again. It may well have been imagination, but the meandering line in the endless black-grey sea of stones would seem a little lighter. More properly, there were several tracks, or lines which looked like tracks, but I went forward as my intuition dictated and the porters followed without demur. The map, a sketch map of the principal ridges, with the most important summits and side valleys, was still stuffed in the pocket of my rucksack. I seldom took it out; it wasn't a lot of help on this terrain. I left it to my instinct to find the route, and when by chance I would come upon an upturned slab, and then a little further on, another, or even an empty tin can, I knew my instinct had not deceived me.

From the top of a rise, I could see back along the glacier for a good distance, and even further forwards. It was not a bit like Nepal – no vegetation; and not like the high Hindu Kush or Aconcagua – quite different colouring. Notwithstanding that, I thought at times of Manaslu in the Central Himalayas, then again of Aconcagua. I knew that such memories could help me, but could just as equally stand in my way.

It may be that I thought the same things, did the same things on the stretch from Liligo to Urdukas, as from Urdukas to here. Certainly it was all very similar – the same moraine hillocks, the same forms – only the mountains to the right and left were different. Everything else was the same as the day before. Was it really still me stamping over the glacier? A little weary from the long march, but not exhausted, swinging my arms and sometimes going for hours on end without thinking of anything in particular. Sometimes my knees gave way if a stone rolled under my feet. My eyes mostly stared blankly at the ground or at some distant object, but not recognising anything. Especially on the long, repetitive, straight stretches, with the pleasant feeling of approaching fatigue, I could forget everything and just keep on going, going, going . . . . In fact I no longer seemed certain where it was I was going to.

"Nirvana" I thought, all day-long nothing but "Nirvana". I said the word over and over "Nirvana – Nirvana – Nirvana – ", the Sanskrit word for transcendentalism, spiritual peace, Final beatitude.

July 21st. Still on the Baltoro. I was waiting for my Baltis in driving snow. It had become too cold to sit on a stone and wait, so I walked round in circles. Some porters coming back from another expedition, approached in the opposite direction. They were looking for empty tins at an earlier camp spot. Three young Baltis with blankets over their heads and shoulders, and over their goatskin sacks. Their feet were wrapped in strips of hide. They went past me without a backward glance. Their ironical smiles revealed what they thought of me –another Sahib like all the others they had come to know in the course of their lives. I watched them go. Whose party had they been with? How long would it take them to get back to their village? five, six, or ten days? Soon they disappeared behind one of the many moraine humps and I gazed absently at nothing.

136

View from Urdukas across the Baltoro Glacier to the granite walls on the (true) right bank of the glacier. In the centre the Trango Massif.

Suddenly, Khaled was standing next to me, followed by our small column of porters. I hadn't noticed him come up. A tough man, this young Khaled, slim and elegant. He now wore climbing breeches, an anorak, thick socks and high military boots. Not because he thought that by wearing them, they made him into a mountaineer, but because they were practical. His black hair always looked freshly combed, even when the wind was blowing. His pace was too irregular and unsteady for a climber, but he was certainly a good soldier.

I had intended to get much further today, but it was too late for the porters had already shed their loads and could not be persuaded to pick them up again. No urging or shouting had any effect. It was snowing and Concordia was still a long way off. The glacier here was very stony and there was no water, only ice to melt. Even when the snow had stopped falling and the sun broke through the clouds, it had no warmth. It merely painted the western flanks of the mountains a light reddish gold for a while, and laid a sheen on the rocks.

We camped on an open ridge, exposed to the icy wind that blew over the glacier. The porters prepared tea. I photographed and talked to

137

The Baltoro Glacier flows like a rough sea of stones from Concordia to Paiju. Fifty kilometres of ice and detritus. A dozen smaller glaciers flow into the main stream.

them. The typical behaviour of a Sahib! First he drives you hard all day, then he wants to sit with you to satisfy his need for human contact.

The porter, to whom an hour below Urdukas I lent my sun hat, winked at me. He wanted to keep the yellow hat, but I refused. He smiled all over his pock-marked face, with his head tilted winningly on one side. "No!" I said, and that was that. I had borrowed the hat from Uschi as I packed for the expedition "Protection against the fierce sun" I argued and promised to bring it back to her. Uschi well knew my habit of bartering with the locals. The porter was not unhappy about this, but sad, like a child can be sad. "Okay" I said. "You can keep it until we get to Base Camp."

138

These Balti-men have the staying power of long distance runners. They have such thin arms and legs, and I believed it was because of this that they could put up with such hardships: they have no fat at all, just muscle, sinews, skin and bones. During our expedition, we never had a porter ill, and they were always in good spirits. Even the one with the yellow hat was in a good mood again.

I lay awake in my tent for half the night.

The morning sun rose behind Gasherbrum IV in a whole spectrum of shades from red to violet-black. As the sun's rays caught the valley floor, every single stone sparkled and the hoar frost melted. The glacier slowly began to come back into life. All its noises – its gurglings and crackings, hummings and rattlings that die down to a murmur at

At Concordia (left) the Baltoro Glacier divides. The right-hand stream flows from the Gasherbrum group, the Godwin Austen Glacier (left) from K2.

night, strike up again as the sun comes up. The air smelt of smoke and turned earth, and where the porters had been, of sweat, fish and rancid butter. How clear the sky was over the mountains. Only a light haze on the horizon. Mitre Peak and Gasherbrum IV dominated the scene.

The fascination of the Baltoro Peaks lies not just in their challenge to mountaineers, their height and difficulty, but also in their very form. One does not need to be a scientist to imagine the elemental forces that went into raising these mighty mountain walls! In the same way as a journey down the Dona Khola or the Modi Khola in the Himalayas, can soon teach you all there is to know about the term 'folded mountains'.

During the afternoon, the sky darkened again. The wispy patches of mist, lighter across the stones, were barely distinguishable from the grey brew above. One could only make out where the glacier met the sky, by the merest brightening of the greyness, and it was no longer possible to determine any colour amongst the stones. Even the tongues of ice, which formerly threaded their way through the debris like glistening veins, were now nothing but lustreless grey patches, covered in smutty snow. As we picked our way around the great boulders, the howl of the wind would rise, then sink again to a mournful lament.

We struggled against the wind, against the driving rain and snow, the ground loose under our feet and the visibility down to almost nothing. I had to hold myself back from plodding blindly ahead of the others, up and down, further and further away. From time to time I

140

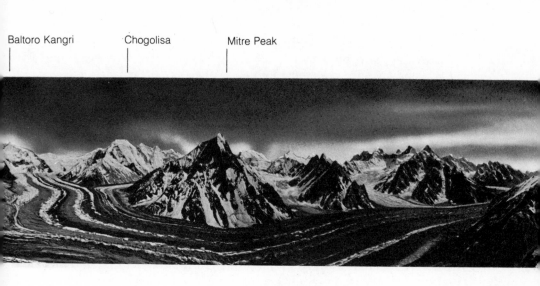

made myself wait until I heard them coming, snatches of conversation in the wind or the sound of stones moving under their feet. Sometimes it was half an hour before their spectral shapes would materialise from the milky mist. It was difficult not to lose heart altogether. The rain turned to snow, but the flakes melted on contact with the damp stones, only settling on the ice. The rising vapours served only to intensify the general feeling of melancholy. The mountains were nowhere to be seen, and nowhere could we find a sheltered campsite.

We had been going till late afternoon before I called a halt beside a rock as large as a house. In no time at all, the porters had brought out their plastic sheets and crawled underneath them, leaving their loads scattered all over the place in the driving sleet. Laboriously I collected them together and stacked them as best I could out of the wet. It was astonishing to see how small a space twelve porters could cram into! So close together, almost on top of each other, they crouched down on the stone-covered ice. Lying in my damp tent, I could hear them moaning and their teeth chattering. Several times I crawled out and gave them what clothing I could spare: duvet jacket, waterproofs, pullover, anorak, bivvy sack – so that those on the outside at least, might have some protection against the cold.

Nights up here were very long, and it was snowing very heavily. What should I do if it was still snowing in the morning? Leave the porters and go on alone, or sit it out? We couldn't withstand another night like this.

141

The weather next morning was not good, but at least it had stopped snowing. Now perhaps I could see where we were. We were quite a way past Concordia, the confluence of half a dozen glaciers which together make the mighty Baltoro. In nine hours from the bivouac, we reached Base Camp – nine hours of rubbly ice and waist-deep, blue-green streams through which we had to wade.

"Long live the crow!"

With this greeting that he had picked up from the American 1963 Everest Expedition, Peter greeted us. He had found an ideal position for our Base Camp, close to that of the Polish Women's Expedition to Gasherbrum III, whom we had supposed would have left for home long before. He reported that the Schell group could not be persuaded to abandon their attempt on Hidden Peak by the ordinary route. Schell was desperately anxious to climb an eight-thousander to round off his list of successes on mountains round the world, to cap this list with such a glittering prize.

That same day we paid off the porters and an hour later, they left Base Camp on their way back to Skardu. We were now alone and must stand on our own feet, dependent on no-one else. Here at 5,000 metres in this remote corner of the world, would begin our most audacious joint venture.

That evening we were invited to share a meal with the Poles, whom we found to be genuinely friendly, cultured people. In their tents we enjoyed classical music, all kinds of games and lively discussion. Their spirits were still high although they had been more than two months on the mountain and overstayed their allocated time. If my theory about national expeditions reflecting the characteristics of the countries from which they come, is correct, then Poland must be a beautiful place to live in.

The next morning I went to see Hans Schell in his Base Camp, which was a good way closer to the mountain than ours.

"Good morning."

The atmosphere was cool. We chatted for a while about this and that. Then, "I hope you understand that we can't agree to your climbing our mountain", I said, bringing the conversation round to the point at issue.

"No, I'm afraid not. We don't have any conscience on that score."

"And no permit either."

"Sadly, no."

I ascended this icefall on the Abruzzi Glacier with our column of porters. This bizarre landscape has not changed for thousands of years

"That's typical! First of all you ask us to give you permission, but you don't stop to think what the consequences might be for us."

"What are you going on about?" Hans seemed embarrassed.

"We have come all this way to climb Hidden Peak alpine-style. That's the understanding on which we partly financed this expedition. Even if you were to tunnel your way to the top from the other side of the mountain, there would still be people who would denounce our efforts and say that we were not alone."

"That's nonsense."

"You amaze me, how naive you are!"

"I can't believe anyone will bat an eyelid if we climb the mountain at the same time from opposite sides. You from the north, we from the south. Even a child could see that we would be two separate outfits, unconnected in any way."

"A child might. But we're talking about people who look for trouble, so they can write sensational articles in alpine periodicals."

"And if no-one tells them?"

I had to laugh. Hans tried to justify his remark.

"We are only on this expedition for ourselves. We have no newspaper contracts and don't want any publicity. We're not accountable to anyone. We came here to climb, that's all. It's not for glory that we want to climb an eight-thousander."

"Very noble sentiments" said I, "But I don't think your good intentions would last long after you had reached the summit!"

"Nobody will hear anything about our expedition, if you don't want them to – not even our families."

"Come off it – I've heard that before. First of all you play it quietly, but before you know it, it's in all the papers. Then it starts raining medals and official speeches. The more you hold back at first, the bigger the hoo-ha later."

"You're wrong, as far as we are concerned."

"What does that mean? It's perfectly natural to tell a reporter when you've done something special, to send a few lines to an alpine journal, or even to receive some award from a local dignitary or alpine club. That's life. You can't pretend it isn't. If we let you climb Hidden Peak, you could write whatever you wanted afterwards, tell whoever you wanted. We couldn't stop you."

"You've got it all wrong. We're only interested in climbing."

"In that case, climb Baltoro Kangri I – that's what you've got your permit for. If you're only interested in climbing, it doesn't matter a damn what the actual height is."

"You jolly well know we want an eight-thousander! Please understand, this might be my last chance – who knows, I could be too old

144

before I get another opportunity."

"I don't know if any other eight-thousander expedition has ever shared its permit. However, I'll do it for your sake, Hans. I leave it up to you. I don't know your friends, they may be very nice people, but it wouldn't be the first time an eight-thousander had turned someone's head, so watch out!"

Hans beamed. We had been very close to hard words, but the high regard I have always felt for this fine, active Styrian climber, one of the most experienced expedition-men in all Austria, was in no way diminished. Both of us, and Peter as well, belonged to the HG Bergland, the high level section of the Vienna branch of the Austrian Alpine Club. And as far as mountaineering goes, we shared similar views.

We shook hands on it and worked out the details. Schell wanted to pay for the permit and help us transport our expedition gear back. He still looked uncertain.

"Would you like all this in writing?" he asked.

"No, it's OK" I said, "I trust you."

I had aired my misgivings but had now agreed to share the permit as a gesture of goodwill. "Will you never learn?", I muttered to myself.

In our little Base Camp, Peter and I made ourselves at home. Khaled had found accommodation with the liaison officers of the other expeditions. Thus his misgivings about remaining alone in camp while Peter and I were on the mountain, were banished.

Partly to acclimatise and partly to have a look at the Northwest Face of Hidden Peak, on July 26th we climbed the two lower Gasherbrum icefalls. This wildly-crevassed hanging glacier, squeezed between Hidden Peak and Gasherbrum VI, led in two stages from our Base Camp up into the Gasherbrum Valley, above which our peak was concealed. (It was not visible beyond the Abruzzi Glacier.)

We were not the first to have scouted a way between these crevasses and seracs. In 1958 it had been the Italians en route for Gasherbrum IV; two years before that, the Austrians under Fritz Moravec going to Gasherbrum II; prior to us in 1975, the French had been to that same summit and the Poles to Gasherbrums III and II. Each group had to find its own way, and we also were forced to adopt our own route to suit the prevailing conditions. In the lower part, the crevasses were open, but the metre-long icicles clinging from the seracs were still well frozen. Early in the morning, the glacier was a safe enough place, but later on as the sun's rays bea. down on it, it would have been suicidal to attempt it. Whole ice towers caved in, and new crevasses opened up; from the faces to the left and right, avalanches thundered down.

Sooner than expected, we reached the flat Gasherbrum Valley, 5,900 metres above sea level. We proposed to bivouac here, take a look at the

Hidden Peak: after twelve days of hard marching I saw our objective for the first time. In the centre of the photo is the western bastion and to the right the IHE-Spur via which the mountain was first climbed in 1958 by an American party (Kauffmann-Schoening). This route was followed by the Schell expedition in 1975.

face in the morning, and then return to Base Camp. All six Gasherbrum summits, which form a compact circle around the valley, are pyramidal in shape. The most impressive of all is Gasherbrum I, or Hidden Peak, our own objective. Its summit wall rises for more than 2,000 metres. Opposite lies the West flank of Gasherbrum II, which together with Gasherbrum III form a vast pyramid. The two peaks are only separated from each other by a saddle at a height of 7,600 metres, and then in their turn, they have the form of two little finely-detailed pyramids. To the west stands the pyramid of Gasherbrum IV, narrow and appallingly steep, then follows Gasherbrums V and VI, both considerably lower, but again both pyramidal ice peaks, the first horn-shaped, the second broader and more squat.

Sitting outside our tent up there, waiting for the sun to go down, I was reminded of the same time last year when Uschi and I had walked from St. Jakob to an isolated farm on an alpine meadow, surrounded by pine forests, with a view over the Villnöss Valley.

"You will be an old man before you realise how much you are missing", she had said. "How many summers, how many springs, how many glorious autumns."

She had been right.

The setting sun bathed the Northwest Face of Hidden Peak in a warm glow. All its ribs stood out in sharp contrast, all its concavities equally clear. Both routes that Peter and I had considered, seemed steeper than they had looked from below. Were they possible? Soon we would know.

A quarter of an hour later, the sun disappeared and there remained nothing but the darkness of another night. Before we made our final attempt, we would climb up here again, and go on as far as the Gasherbrum Col, in order to get a view of our face in profile and to ascertain where the worst avalanche runnels and stonefalls were, so that we could select the safest possible route. After this second reconnaissance, we would attempt the face in a single push, bottom to top.

Back in Base Camp, the rustlings and cracklings of the stones falling from the edge of the moraine into the crevasses, the gurgling and piping of underground streams beneath our tent, the sight of the ever-moving, ever-reshaping white mist, became so commonplace to Peter and me, that we took no notice. For a week we had been installed on the Abruzzi Glacier and were now ready to make our second reconnaissance.

When Peter woke me at first light, it was frosty and damp in the tent. Reluctantly I dressed, stepped outside and stretched my legs. The sky was clear and a light breeze wafted from the Conway Saddle. We drank tea, put on our heavy packs which we had got ready the night before, and began our climb over the icefall. We again made use of our first bivouac site. The view from the Gasherbrum Col the next morning revealed that the righthand route – which was menaced by a huge serac at around 7,200 metres – was out of the question. So the lefthand route it had to be. We descended to Base Camp again.

View over the Abruzzi Glacier to Concordia. Our tiny Base Camp lies to the right in a corner between the rocks.

THE SUMMIT BID

August 5th, Uschi's birthday. I sat in Base Camp at the foot of Hidden Peak, wishing I could be with her. Since our departure from Munich Airport four weeks ago, I had heard nothing from her. When the weather was bad, I often lay in my tent for hours on end, asking myself why we were here and what it was we wanted, and finding no answers. But if I put the questions aside and read a book or went for a walk along the moraine, I would stop worrying and it would all be clear to me once more. When I was doing something, working consciously towards an end anticipating the summit attempt, I could see a purpose in it all.

The weather seemed to run to a set pattern: three or four days bad, three or four days good. It was clear that we must make the most of the very next good weather period and launch a determined effort on the summit. Our rucksacks were ready. Again and again, we had unpacked and repacked them. A single pound overweight could cost us success, and a small thing omitted could be equally disastrous.

Peter and I had to carry everything ourselves. There were no fixed ropes on the face, no prepared high camps. Although we had settled on the route we would follow, we had not, so far, put a foot on the face itself.

When, as now, the wind dispelled the mist, we could see Chogolisa from Base Camp, a beautiful white snow and ice peak, shaped like the roof of a house. It was on Chogolisa, after having climbed Broad Peak in 1957, that Hermann Buhl attempted on a seven-thousander what we now hoped to do on an eight-thousander. Together with Kurt Diemberger, the greatest living Austrian expedition-mountaineer, he endeavoured, moving the tent from bivouac site to bivouac site, to climb the mountain without any outside help. The two-man rope operated in West Alpine style. But just below the summit, the weather suddenly changed. They began to descend right away, but somehow, Buhl must have stepped too close to the corniced edge; the snow gave way and he disappeared for ever.

From our 'Bath Room', a crack dug in the ice, I could see the finely-

Hermann Buhl introduced the Western Alps style of climbing to the Himalayas. His Broad Peak expedition of 1957 carried a total weight of 2000kg whereas we made do with 200kg on Hidden Peak.

chiselled ridge of Chogolisa.

"Up there – that must be the spot where it happened", I thought, and into my mind came the image of Buhl's wife and his three daughters. This charming, capable lady had learned to cope with widowhood, and her daughters were now grown-up.

"Have you ever thought of trying the South Face of Dhaulagiri?" Peter brought me out of my reverie.

"Dhaulagiri South Face? That would be worth a try! But not for two men, you would need four for that. It must be the highest face in the Nepal Himalaya, 4,000 metres or more. Steep and concave like the Eigerwand, but wider."

"Do you think you could get a permit?"

"Perhaps – I'll try it and see. But there's always the problem of finding a team and financing it all, of course."*

I lay awake in the tent for hours. I kept remembering all sorts of people – why, I don't know. Perhaps it was fear. At last I pulled myself together and went outside. As I looked around I noticed that the summits of Gasherbrum II and Hidden Peak were clear of mist. Had the weather changed for the better? Could we make a start tomorrow? Back in my sleeping bag, I looked at my watch – not 'tomorrow' but today. It was already past midnight.

It suddenly occurred to me that I had seen all fourteen of the eight-

*In the meantime, the permit has been obtained. In 1977 Reinhold Messner will attempt Dhaulagiri South Face with a four-man team.

thousand metre peaks – and I counted them off in my head, first west to east, then in the reverse direction from Kangchenjunga, back to Nanga Parbat. As I lay there, the images of these fourteen mountains came to me – K2 from Concordia – how the mists had rolled around this huge pyramid, enshrouding, then revealing it. That was on the march-in two weeks ago. Nearby was Broad Peak, the last to catch the setting sun; the name says it all – broad, mighty.

Over the Nuptse-Lhotse Wall, the summit ridge of Everest. Not so spectacular as I had imagined, but the highest mountain in the world nevertheless, and for that reason, somewhat unbelievable and fascinating.

Makalu. That was pre-monsoon 1974 I had been there. From the first camp I had often gazed up its well-proportioned South Face. How the wind raged up there! Kilometre-long snow plumes on the ridge. I could visualise again, the column of porters marching in, Camp I, Camp II, Camp III and the blizzard on the summit wall. This was too much, I ought to get to sleep . . . .

Hardly had I closed my eyes, before new peaks floated before me. Nanga Parbat! How often had I been to Nanga? 1970, 1971, 1973, 1974. I knew it from all sides – better than all the other eight-thousanders put together. In my imagination, the mountain pivoted before me; buttress after buttress, ridge after ridge. I examined its every detail. Summit, South Shoulder, North Shoulder, Rakiot Peak, Silver Saddle. I let the mists enfold it once more, then conjured it up again, but the summit pitches only this time. I tried to introduce myself into the picture, on the top of the mountain, but it didn't work. No-one would be visible from this distance. The final solitude cannot be fabricated; that has to be born each time anew.

Whenever I tried to picture Manaslu, always it was the storm that came to my mind first of all; but there were photos I could reconstruct, photos that I had taken of its complicated southern elevation.

Suddenly, Dhaulagiri was there, Dhaulagiri from Gorapani, Dhaulagiri from the south. What a face! And Annapurna from the north, from Tilicho Peak – all those sloping snow fields.

Classical expeditions to Eight thousanders today cost from DM 300,000 to 500,000. hundred porters were necessary on Lhotse to carry the 18 tons of expedition equipment Base Camp. On Hidden Peak we had 12 porters and 200 kg weight of equipment. Cost, r including flying, about DM10,0

(top left) Camp I (6000 m) on Lhotse. Ama Dablam in the backgroun
(top right) The second bivouac on Hidden Peak. Masherbrum to the right re
(bottom left) On the way to Hidden Peak. Baltoro Kangri in the backgrou
(bottom right) On route for Lhotse. Island Peak in the backgroun

It was a good 100 km from Askole, the last village, to Base Camp on Hidden Peak: glacier streams, bivouacs in the open air – a desolate area of ice and detritus, surrounded by fascinating mountains.

I counted them up: Gasherbrum II, Hidden Peak, K2, Broad Peak, Lhotse, Everest, Makalu, Nanga, Manaslu, Dhaulagiri, Annapurna. That only made eleven. I went through them again. Then I remembered my flight over Katmandu in 1972. Far in the north in the crystal morning light, I had seen the outline of Shisha Pangma, the Chinese eight-thousander. Then there was Kangchenjunga, seen in 1974 from Cogma La; nearer and darker than Shisha Pangma, but still too far away to pick out any fine detail. I was still one short. Oh yes, Cho Oyu, seen on our march-in to Lhotse. An astonishing massif – someone really ought to try and get a permit to attempt it from the south. That tilted spur cried out for a route.

I had been through them all, all the eight-thousanders, but still sleep eluded me. I tried to take my mind off the mountains and think of home. All that came to mind was Gshmagenhart, a peaceful alm at the foot of the Geislerspitzen. It was from here I had made my first excursions into the mountains with my parents.

At that moment the first glimmers of morning light broke into my reminiscences. Time to get going!

The glacier was fairly quiet. The streams that one could hear gurgling through the crevasses when the sun shone, were still frozen. The avalanche channels still safe, and the seracs as firm as houses. Icicles did not break off, unless we touched them. The only sounds as we climbed the lower icefall were the soft crunching of the frozen snow under our boots and the swishing as our gaitered boots rubbed together. All the crevasses were open. We knew them well from our two previous reconnaissances, and didn't bother with the rope. Peter took up the rear, and I went on ahead, taking care not to lose the right way.

I looked up at the stars, which at times seemed to be paling already, at times still glittering coldly. It promised to be a clear, fine day. Soon the dawn gave way to a glassy blue light, and the two summit ridges of Chogolisa acquired a warm glow. Peter and I forged ahead easily even though our rucksacks were loaded down with pegs, ropes, crampons, food, stoves, sleeping bags. We carried more than 20 kilos each.

We did not speak, finding the silence of these early hours, soothing. We absorbed the peace into ourselves. The feelings of anxiety and inevitability that had troubled me at times the night before, had now completely vanished, replaced by a happy self-confidence that has accompanied the start of all my big climbs. Every muscle felt fit, and as I moved from one step to the next in the icefall, or when I jumped over the crevasses, my confidence grew. Our legs coped tirelessly with each

Our porters climbing competently over the rocks above the Braldo River. A single slip would pitch them into the torrent.

contour of the glacier. The morning wind blew the last traces of sleep from my beard and hair. I didn't seem to notice the weight of my rucksack, which was piled higher than my head.

Peter concentrated in turn on the route, then on his legs, which seemed to have been provided with springs. Without consciously thinking about it, I realised how important these simple experiences are at the beginning of a big climb. With each step our strength and determination grew. But equally I knew that in the final analysis strength and endurance were not enough; it was strength of purpose and a belief in our enterprise, that really counted.

Peter had caught up and was standing beside me,

"I think it will go, Reinhold" he said.

"Yes, if the weather holds."

"It must!"

I broke off the conversation and began climbing again, anxious to recover my rhythm. Without resting again, we climbed a series of steep ice steps and quickly reached the basin above the first icefall. From here the glacier ascended evenly and levelled out into the Gasherbrum Valley, bounded to the left and right by mighty rock and ice walls.

For a few minutes, we set our rucksacks down and sat on them. As we rested there in silence, contemplating the peaks on the other side of the valley, the sun rose far behind Sia Kangri. We couldn't see it, but its first rays picked out the hollows and ridges of Baltoro Kangri, a squat ice dome between Chogolisa and Sia Kangri. In the feeble reflected light, the rocks and snow patches on the west side of Hidden Peak, below which we were now sitting, appeared uniformly grey and disjointed.

A few metres above our rest spot, a long, wide crevasse crossed the glacier; our first serious difficulty of the morning. We decided to rope up. I took twenty metres of rope from my rucksack, found my harness and tied on to the water-repellent perlon rope. Peter did the same, donning a sit-harness so that he would not be asphyxiated under the pressure of the rope, should he fall into the crevasse. Having completed these routine precautions, we took up our rucksacks again. Only then we noticed for the first time how heavy they were. I shuffled the weight about a bit till it was more comfortable, and walked along the edge of the crevasse on a tight rope. Peter followed, at a distance of about 20 metres. Hoping to find a place where we could easily jump across, we traversed a fair way to the right.

Peter and I had shared out the few pegs and ice screws we had brought with us, so that either of us could free himself from a crevasse, if need be, whilst the other belayed him. We had a tacit understanding that we would exchange leads, sharing the work of the route finding and belaying.

158

By now it was 7 a.m. The sun shone, as it did only on crystal-clear days, like a great, bright wedge in the Upper Gasherbrum Valley, where it joined the west face of Gasherbrum V. It wasn't long before we heard the thundering of the first avalanches. Peter and I were still in shadow; I hesitated a moment, then sprang over the crevasse, which was now only two metres wide. For safety's sake, Peter had first withdrawn from the edge, rammed his pick in the hard-frozen snow, and promised to pay the rope out carefully, without jerking it. As I landed on the other side, I threw myself forward, driving my axe firmly into the snow at the same time, so that I could hold myself if I slipped. The crevasse was seemingly bottomless, with shattered ice clinging to its sides. I shivered involuntarily as I bent forward and peered inside. Then I stepped back a few metres, plunged the shaft of my axe into the snow, took in the rope and safeguarded Peter's leap over the crevasse.

Now we went on upwards, still in shadow. During the day when the sun was full on them, these glacier valleys were extraordinarily dangerous. Fresh crevasses opened up, seracs collapsed and the general going was much more difficult. But climbing before the sun had had a chance to soften the snow, was not too bad. Here and there we sank in up to our ankles, but mostly the snow was so hard that the soles of our boots left practically no trace on its surface. It was not yet necessary to use crampons, for the smooth ice showed only rarely through the snow covering and was easy to avoid.

We were about half way up a gently sloping snow field when the sun first reached us. The light was dazzling and we had to stop and put our dark glasses on. For a time we maintained the same direction, then turned right between gigantic serac towers and followed the right-hand edge of the icefall. There we crossed – as we had on our reconnaissance trips – a steep, avalanche-prone slope and reached the Gasherbrum Valley, where we intended to bivouac. We still had sufficient time and energy to climb further up the valley as far as to the foot of the Northwest Face of Hidden Peak, but we preferred to spend the night in our accustomed place. We knew what the wind was like there and that the basin was safe from avalanches; in emergency, we could evacuate quickly and make a safe retreat to Base Camp.

The sun was still burning down. It shone right onto the roof of our tent with such ferocity that we were obliged to drape our sleeping bags over it, to make it bearable inside. We partly unpacked our rucksacks and left them outside the tent.

Peter was plagued with such a bad headache, he had to lie down and take a pain-killer, and try to sleep it off. It lasted for hours; his head felt as if it would burst. He not only had difficulty in speaking, but also found it hard to breathe. He lay there, as still as he could, staring at the tent roof and groaning. I tried to prepare him some tea in a little aluminium pot, and had difficulty in keeping the gas cooker upright so that the water didn't spill. I gave Peter some of the warm drink and he sipped it slowly, then tried again to go to sleep. But despite the tea and lying absolutely still, the headache persisted. In his weakened and lonely condition, he began to be troubled by a deep inner disquiet. He could picture his friend Regina standing before him, and recalled everything he could about her and how she had sailed for South Africa, where she now lived a new life amongst strange people. Peter tried to remember the first time they had spoken to each other and why they were now apart, why she had gone away. He wanted to bring back his happiest memories of their relationship, and in so doing, he fell asleep.

I too must have slept a while. We didn't wake up until the sun had disappeared behind Gasherbrum V and it was cold inside the tent. Peter's headache had lifted and he was ready again for action, convinced that we could succeed. The setting sun winked through the gap between Gasherbrums V and VI and cast its glow on Hidden Peak.

Again we drank some tea. Although I took great care to hold my mug steady, I still slopped some of the hot drink over my fingers, occasioning a sharp, lingering pain. My fingers were now icy cold, and where I had scalded them, had turned white.

Later, still in front of the tent, we emptied out our rucksacks and sorted through everything again. We put aside some things we didn't think we should need, like spare gas cartridges, some food and a number of pitons. Our sacks should now weigh around 13 kilos each. We could not settle down until we had them packed ready, then we stuck our axes in the snow and hung the rope over the tent door. My feelings alternated between pleasant anticipation and a certain misgiving about the severity and danger of our impending enterprise. The sun had now gone down as we stood side by side under the darkening sky in the cold evening wind. It was quite dark when we finally retreated into the tent.

We made ourselves as comfortable as we could in the narrow tent, and brewed up some more tea. Drinking was more important than anything else. We had to tank up on fluids as we wouldn't have any during the next day. It would take too much time and effort to carry water or tea with us.

For a while I watched over Peter's shoulder as he cooked and busied himself with the pots and pans. The soup was hot and very salty. The bread was so hard it creaked as we chewed it. It had been a present from a Villnöss farmer – iron rations for the summit bid. This home-made farm bread was nutritious and satisfying, ideal for an eight-thousander. We chatted as we ate, encouraging each other in the

160

thought that by this time tomorrow, the worst of the face should be behind us. Success now depended on our condition, and whether or not we were sufficiently acclimatised. Our actual climbing skills ought to be adequate to cope with anything we should find on the face. In the Alps, we had climbed very much harder faces, albeit at much lower altitudes.

Climbing is like cycling or swimming, once you have learned it, you never forget it. What you do have to do each year, is to build up your balancing powers, and above all, your condition. You need great strength in your thighs and calves, and also in the forearms and fingers, which are of tremendous importance on steep and overhanging terrains.

We were both aware that this climb was breaking new ground. Neither of us had ever before attempted a high mountain without support from below, and even if the climbing difficulties were no greater than on other expeditions or alpine routes, we still had to face up to the fact that we were completely alone, without the moral support of a back-up team. We had no doctor and not the slightest hope that anyone would rescue us if anything should go wrong.

The middle section of Hidden Peak's North Face is incredibly steep, as steep perhaps as the Matterhorn North Face. When Peter and I thought about it, that it could perhaps be just shattered rock, we weren't sure if our courage would stretch to climbing it. An experienced mountaineer can climb a rotten face, only so long as it is not overhanging, and only if the hand and foot holds can be used just as pressure holds. His instinct would prevent him from pulling up on a loose hold, or moving out of balance; if he maintained his flow of movement and didn't jerk about here and there, he could get up. We both knew this and had often practised it; the only question was, whether we could translate alpine techniques up here to seven or eight thousand metres above sea level. Technique alone is not enough at these heights – willpower and endurance are equally important factors. We would also need confidence in ourselves, if we were to bear this last, boundless loneliness. We now had to estimate the difficulties and steepness of the face to enable us to prepare for all eventualities; and we had to work out the actual detailed route from stance to stance. A slip on the face could mean curtains for one or both of us. So although we knew basically what line we would follow, it was up to us tomorrow to work it out exactly, and to always know where we wanted to be and where the next usable hold might be.

Peter and I luckily both have an instinct for picking the right line. That is our strength. We were probably no better climbers than many others – although it is true we had as much experience as a dozen or

161

more good climbers put together – but that was not the decisive factor. What we had both developed, gradually over 25 years of climbing, was this kind of instinct, which didn't desert us even if we were exhausted or under stress. What we had more than others, was this combination of ability, experience and a mutual trust that knew practically no bounds.

In the next few days, we must not allow ourselves one false move, nor one miscalculation, for the one would surely lead to death and the other to demoralisation and defeat. When climbing in the Alps, a fall often only results in scraped knees and elbows, or a broken bone if you hit something, but up above 7,000 metres, one could not hope to be so lucky. A fall would not only result in suffering considerable shock, which at this altitude would be dangerous in itself, but it would also involve loss of strength; even if no injury was involved, one man would not be able to rescue the other, and he certainly could not carry him down the mountain. With even the least mishap, we should be trapped.

All this I thought as I lay in the tent trying to sleep. The fact that I was able to think these possibilities through to their logical ends, without frightening myself too much, was evidence that my self-confidence ran high and that Peter was the best partner possible for such a hazardous venture.

'Lali guras' suddenly came into my mind. It was the name of a rhododendron. I couldn't imagine why I should suddenly think of it. "Lali guras Mam Sahib" was the name the Sherpas had given to a girl on one of my trekking tours. I wished I could go to sleep like the Tibetan dogs on the way home to Europe. Do dogs understand Yoga? I have practised Yoga myself, but eight hours of total relaxation, that I haven't managed yet! My thoughts now winged to Uschi. How I would have liked to stand on the summit of Hidden Peak for her birthday. An eight-thousander is no kind of birthday present, but it would mean I could be back with her the sooner.

I thought of the dogs again – Yeti, who had been with us for more than a year, pepper-and-salt coloured, jealous, but the most intelligent of the three; Taschi, the jumping bitch, who used to amaze even the Tibetans when, with her bright eyes and soft paws, she stood on her back legs and salaamed 'Namaste'; then there was Jakbu, who was clumsy, charming, impetuous, trusting – all at the same time. He even liked children, which is unusual with these dogs. Would they recognise me when I got home, I wondered.

Hidden Peak from the north.

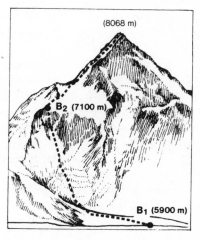

.....Messner-Habeler Route.

B1 = First bivouac.
B2 = Second bivouac.

163

THE FACE

The route we had chosen lies somewhat to the east of the fall-line below the ice bulge that projects from the lower section of the Northwest Face. In our opinion this was the only possible line of ascent, besides being the most direct.

We threw our rucksacks into the snow, put on our crampons and roped up. Although the rocks projecting from the centre of the face were already in the sun, the gullies remained quiet so we did not fear stonefalls. Only once, as I was hanging from an ice screw in a bulging serac, coiling the rope, did a few fragments of rock and ice shoot down the Gasherbrum Face, hissing into the snow at the foot of the climb. The surface of the snow below the bergschrund was level and without crevasses, so we had no trouble crossing it. Our boot soles did not penetrate more than a few millimetres into the hard snow surface, and to start with, the going was not particularly strenuous.

We passed quickly through the Gasherbrum Valley, and it was glorious to see the sun slowly flooding the walls to our left. The view that now faced us was a breathtaking one – we stood directly between two eight-thousanders.

We advanced a few steps, then Peter offered me a piece of chocolate and we stopped to tighten our crampons. All the time we could hear a curious sound that vibrated all around. During the last few hours, as we were marching up the Gasherbrum Valley, this kind of humming had been getting stronger. Our regular steps had not disturbed it, and only when we spoke briefly at the rest pauses, did we cease to hear it. This sound did not come from the wind, nor was it due to fresh crevasses opening up, but rather, it came from the mountain itself. From the whole surroundings. From the snow and ice and rock and out of the air, even, which still seemed to be frozen in the narrow valley. It is a sound I have heard before but never experienced so intensely as now. It is the sound of silence, the accompaniment to solitude. Peaceful. I was well aware of the objective dangers that faced us, but felt neither anxiety nor agitation. I was hopeful and completely dominated by the sound, which seemed to carry me along.

I looked at Peter to see if he felt the same way. His movements showed that he too was confident, in his element. Only his face was pensive and his eyes somewhat wary. It was easy to see that his whole body was tense with expectation.

With many climbers, the act of climbing extinguishes all other sensations. For them there is no tension, no fear, no yesterday and no tomorrow – wherever they happen to be climbing. When they are on a face, nothing else exists for them – neither the valley below, nor their own life in the valley – simply nothing. Such contentment and unconcern takes possession of me too when I climb and when it goes well.

For as long as we were walking through the Gasherbrum Valley early in the morning, the world seemed to consist of nothing but the snow I crushed under my feet, the walls that rose steeply to left and right of me, the ice axe, the rucksack, and the rhythm I dared not break. But now as we stood at the foot of our wall and prepared to make the ascent, the old worries and fears came flooding back. Perhaps the weather would break tomorrow? It so often does here, suddenly and unexpectedly, and it would be fearfully difficult to find our way back in mist and new snow. We needed at least one more day to descend the face again, and another two or three to Base Camp if we were faced with a storm in the icefall. The fact that the weather was glorious now, did not rule out the possibility of a reversal in five, or seven, or ten hours time. We were too near our first bivouac site at the moment to have any real fears – here it would be a simple matter to retreat to Base Camp. But higher up, if the weather broke, it would be much more difficult. We would need to watch out for avalanche danger and would not be able to descend if avalanches did threaten. Sudden changes of the weather come much more quickly at great heights and storms are much fiercer. But perhaps the weather would hold until we were at the top. At such high altitudes it was sometimes months, it could be years, before a warm, wind-free day would guarantee a safe descent. So it was necessary to be more deliberate and at the same time, more determined, than in the Alps.

Meanwhile, we adjusted our crampons for the third time and again checked our equipment. Everything was OK. We took up our rucksacks, grasped our axes and approached the actual face, purposefully.

If we hoped for success, we must climb steadily; we could only make the actual summit thrust from a higher bivouac.

"Each to climb at his own pace", said Peter.

I nodded, "You go first, then I'll take a turn in front."

"I think we'll make it. If the weather holds for two days, we'll do it."

We changed the lead at regular intervals, the man in front determining the way, the other utilising his footsteps. In this way, the second had a rest from breaking the trail before it was his turn again. It was not always obvious which was the best way, but we trusted each other's navigation implicitly. We did not need to talk; it would have interfered with our regular breathing.

Peter's foot stuck out from the blank ice slope immediately above my head. The top layer of the ice was so soft that the front points of the crampons sank right up to the boot caps, but hard enough to afford a safe stance. Good conditions. Because of our triple boots, the leverage required while climbing, boot toe to heel, was much greater than usual, and the strain on the calf muscles was enormous. After every 25 steps or so, we rested. Peter cut a small step in the ice, and as soon as his right foot was firmly on the hold, he rammed the shaft of his axe well in. Then he leaned his trunk against the ice, holding on hard to his axe, and took a breather. He waited till I had worked my way up to his ledge, and then we climbed another 25 paces.

"What's the ice like up there?" I called to him.

"Better. Crusty."

Peter now contemplated the broken band above him, "But the rock looks bad."

I had already noticed lower down that there were lighter patches on the face.

Coming to a stance, I stuffed a handful of snow into my mouth, leant against my rammed-in axe, and rested. I had always known that Peter would be the ideal man for high altitudes, and now he was proving me right. He climbed steadily and automatically, even when he was getting tired. I was convinced that if a way existed to the summit, he would find it.

"Do you want to rest?" asked Peter, "There's a good place to stand here."

"No. Let's keep going", I replied "so long as the face is out of the sun, we should make the most of it."

Peter was in complete agreement. For although one could never totally discount the risk of stonefalls, in the morning when all the rocks were frozen above us, the going was very much safer than in the afternoon. We did not want to court more danger than was necessary.

In the warmth of the midday sun, more and more ice fragments, rock and scree began to move and were soon hurtling down the slightly concave wall in great bounds. It was impossible to tell which way they would come. Because of the steepness of the face, we were unable to make any quick movements. We had no choice but to wait until the missiles were almost immediately above us, and then twist out of their path. In the Alps, one would normally climb a face like this at night. But here it was too cold at night, and moreover we would probably not have been able to find the ideal way in the dark.

How insignificant and solitary are two men alone on an eight-thousander! Had we stopped to think about it, we would doubtless have been quite worried about the situation in which we now found ourselves. But we kept on climbing this 2,000 metre wall, tirelessly step by step upwards, concentrating only on the 25 steps between the last resting place and the next, rather than on the wall as a whole.

"We must have done 200 metres", I calculated.

"Yeah. Perhaps even 250."

.From Peter's words, I felt that he too was pleased with our tempo. Despite that, it would still take eight or ten hours to reach our next bivouac place. The wall was growing steeper all the time, and far above our heads, projected a series of overhangs, which seemed to bar all possible progress. But – and this we knew from our observations down in the Gasherbrum Valley – we needed to get above these overhangs to find a flatter slope where we could pitch our tent. The cliff plunged steeply away beneath us, and reared above with no terraces or ledges of any size. We prayed that the snow cover would not get any thicker – it was much more exhausting to make tracks through deep snow than to climb blank ice.

Ice climbing on the lower part of the North West Face of Hidden Peak.

I tried to photograph Peter who was climbing directly below me, but I couldn't manage it. I had difficulty putting my camera back into its canvas case, lined with space foil, then I glanced down at Peter again. "Crazy", I thought, "It's simply crazy how he's coming up there. I must have that on film."

It wasn't just awkward, but quite dangerous, to pull the camera out of the rucksack and operate it. At all costs I had to keep my balance, and therefore I leant the upper part of my body against the face. The smallest give of the right foot, which stood in a small notch, the slightest twist of the body, and I ran the risk of falling down the face.

Very, very slowly, but deliberately, we made progress. The twenty-fifth step, the last before each rest pause, seemed like hell, but after a few minutes to recover our breath, we were once more climbing upwards. By now we had more than half of the first sweep of the face, behind us; if we could do the second half as quickly, we should reach our bivouac above the broken band. So we went calmly on, inching our way up. We kept changing the lead, encouraging each other, and gradually put the wall, step by step, behind us. Sometimes just one of us climbed, often we climbed together, one behind the other. Perhaps it was our mutual trust that let us dispense with the usual safety precautions of rope and pegs; or it may have been that our obsession with the idea of a two-man eight-thousander ascent, in part contributed to this unorthodox style of climbing. But more than that, it was the instinctive knowledge that under these circumstances, we were not capable of carrying all the necessary rope and pegs for textbook tactics. Probably ours was the only method that a party of two could reach such a summit by. It was in fact less dangerous than an outside observer might think.

Suddenly, some lumps of ice grazed my left hand, with which I was balanced against the slope. Something must have happened. I looked up at Peter. He was cursing because his foothold had broken away, but he kept on climbing. In no way put out by this slight mishap, he recovered his rhythm immediately. He was climbing in such a manner that he could keep his balance even if he suddenly did lose one of the three points of contact he needed whilst making each move. So long as we kept two firm holds, we would not fall, but all the same, we took care to have three before making each new move.

Meanwhile, we had come directly under the rock step which projected from the wall at 6,900 metres. We debated how best to tackle it, and noticed some gullies fanning out from the concave ice field, like spider's legs into the broken rock. After we had rested on some wide snow steps, which we had scraped out of the slope with our crampons, I made an attempt to climb this first rock band. The rock was completely shattered, but not quite vertical, so that for the most part, I found I could rely on pressure holds. After only a few moves, it was obvious to me that I would have to take off my gloves, and I headed for a steep, but quite big foothold, where it was possible to stand up without holding on. I took off first the left glove and put it in the front pocket of my anorak, then the right. Then with my bare hands, I took a grip in a small crack. The rock was cold but not so icy that one's fingers clove to it, as they did to metal on ice axes and karabiners for instance. An unpleasant feeling. I always expected to leave a piece of skin behind whenever I took my hands off my axe.

Peter, who was holding fast onto the rock with outstretched arms, was watching me intently. After the first few moves on this broken rock, I didn't hesitate but kept moving slowly, traversing to the right. With the palms of my hands pressed flat against the slightly protruding rock, and the points of my crampons dug deep into the loose slope, I shifted my weight centimetre by centimetre, testing first with my hands, then moving when I believed I could safely do so. Although climbing completely free, my body trembling owing to the exertion at this altitude, I remained calm. I felt so much in contact with Peter that it was as if he had me secured on a rope. I had to keep jamming my fists into small cracks filled with fine snow, which unavoidably stuck to my warm skin, and gradually the cold and snow robbed me of all feeling in my fingers. A long rest here would only dissipate my remaining strength, so I kept going, despite the state of my hands. To the right I spied an ice gully which might prove a suitable resting place. There I hoped I should be able to put my gloves back on. I was sure that Peter would be able to climb this pitch, and I followed his progress with the same concentration as he had watched over mine. There was not the slightest sign of uncertainty in his movements, and although his teeth were chattering with cold, not a suspicion of disquiet crossed his face. Instinctively his fingertips found the right cracks, clasped the rock bulges. He kept his weight over the front points of his crampons to prevent them from suddenly slipping.

I took a few deep breaths and began to climb the gully above the rocks. I could not tell yet where it led. A quick look over my shoulder indicated that Peter had safely negotiated the traverse, and was now, breathing heavily, occupying the stance I had just vacated. His forehead pressed against his forearm, he leant heavily against the rock, gasping. Unwittingly, I thought how difficult it would have been to belay here on this crumbling rock. There were no crevices suitable for taking pegs, a large piton would have split the rock and a small one would simply not have held.

Peter in the meantime had got his gloves out of his pocket and put

169

them back on. His hands no longer hurt for he had lost all feeling in them. How he managed that ticklish traverse with his hands in that condition, he was not able to say.

Leaning my head right back, I gazed upwards; the sky was a matt white with a blue background. Out on the horizon where it met the snowy crests, the blue was even mistier. The western facing snow slopes sparkled brilliantly. The view towards the sun was unbearable. Below us, the valleys were visible in a bluish haze, blue with a touch of violet in it, an almost magical effect. Here and there the mist appeared to be bubbling, as if the earth below was boiling. As I hung, poised between heaven and earth, it seemed that there were unfathomable depths below, unfathomable heights above. We were 1,200 metres from the summit, more than 2,000 metres from the valley bottom. My thoughts swam like the blue haze beneath me – another 200 metres and we shall be safe.

The gully narrowed into a chimney. With legs spread wide, I straddled up the crack. The rock was sounder here. I didn't care to think whether or not I could save myself if I were to slip. So I pressed more firmly with my hands against the parallel sides of the chimney. If I were to slip only a short distance, I must surely take Peter with me. He could never have held me if I fell. The chimney now narrowed, which was a piece of luck; it was now easier to wedge ourselves into it.

I continued up another gully until I came to a ridge on my left, and climbing onto this, I reached the shoulder between the North and Northwest Faces. Here I rested. A steep wall now reared above me, rocky in places, all its hollows filled with packed snow. It looked as if it could avalanche at any minute. I was undecided whether or not to go on, and consoled myself that once over this steep rise, we should find our next bivouac spot.

Peter had now joined me, and began at once working his way along the shoulder to the steep snow wall. Here he stopped a moment to summon fresh strength and courage, then made the first moves. First he stuck his axe in the snow, taking a firm hold on the pick with his right hand, and with his left, grasped one of the rocks that protruded like little islands out of the snow; he pulled himself upwards. His arm quivered with effort. After seemingly-endless seconds, he found a small hold for his left crampon under the snow, and shifted his whole weight onto this invisible support. The snow was loose but not too deep. As quickly as the altitude allowed, he climbed obliquely upwards, ramming his axe far above him in the snow so that, holding on to it firmly he could take three steps one after the other. This was a

The 'shattered band' — a steep belt of rock between 6900 and 7100m, was the key section of the North West Face of Hidden Peak. It consisted of verglased and broken rock.

fairly dangerous manoeuvre. He had now reached a flat slab of rock and sat down to wait for me to catch him up. He had done a good job, and hoped that we would be able to use the same tracks for the descent.

"Shall I go ahead now", I asked, as I approached his slab, but my question came too late. Peter was already climbing and from his skilful moves I could see he was just as alert as he had been first thing in the morning.

On these last steep stretches, my legs often got the shakes, especially when I had to stand on just the front points of my crampons.

From where we were, neither of us could see what lay ahead. As Peter's head came level with the top of the ridge and he took the first look over, he shouted excitedly that there was a flat basin up there which would make an ideal bivouac site. I climbed round a rock projection and reached the hold from where he had started his last pitch. Peter's beaming smile over the top of the ridge convinced me that we had climbed enough for one day, and the bivouac site was more than satisfactory. The exertion in gaining the 1,200 metres of height this day had been enormous, yet the strain of it had already lifted from Peter's face, although he was no longer moving as effortlessly as he had been at the beginning of the climb. With the trained eye of an experienced climber, he looked around for the flattest spot in the basin, and it wasn't long before we were both able to stretch ourselves out on a sloping gravelly patch at 7,000 metres.

I settled my rucksack under my head and relaxed instinctively, going quite limp and breathing deeply. I glanced at Peter beside me, wanting to say something, but he had his eyes closed and seemed from his expression, not to have a care in the world. So I shut my eyes too and lay there motionless. After ten hours of strenuous exertion, it was marvellous just to lie and forget the wall beneath us. No need to watch out, no need to find the way, no need to climb any more – at least not tonight.

Our mental tiredness was greater than that of our bodies. We had been in a state of constant tension all day, consciously maintaining our balance and testing the holds by which we had steadily inched our way up, like two mountain locomotives.

On arrival at Base Camp (5100 m) on the Abruzzi Glacier, we paid off the porters and sent them home. We were now completely self-reliant, no longer dependant on anyone else. A height of 3,000m lay between us and the summit.

(top) Base Camp. The western bastion of Hidden Peak behind.
(bottom) The porters took 12 days from Skardu to Base Camp and 8 days for the return journey.

filmed the ascent of the North Face of
idden Peak as far as the difficult
rrain allowed.

A tiny tent weighing 3kg, Perlon
outside and silk inside, was carried up
the 1200m wall to a height of 7100m.
Here we spent our last night before the
summit assault. This tent was destroyed
by a storm the night after the summit
ascent.

"The worst is behind us now", I said, turning round and casting a glance up the summit wall. It was 1,000 metres to the highest point, but it was less steep than the section we had already climbed. And we had the whole night in front of us to recuperate, to regain our strength. "We'll be all right", said Peter, attempting with his boot to smooth out the stones underneath him; the crampons got in his way, so he took them off. "But we can't go down the rocks the same way", he added positively.

"If we can find a crack, we can climb straight down, otherwise we'll have to . . . ."

Peter broke in. "We should have brought a rope."

"We'll get down OK. After the summit, we'll find a way down somehow or other." I was convinced that if there was no other possibility, we could in fact climb down the rocks again without a rope. Peter was not entirely happy at the thought of the descent, but said no more. He'd got his crampons off now and was squatting on his haunches constructing a platform. He placed the largest stones on the outside edge of the patch, kicking the smaller ones after them with his feet, building up a little wall and enlarging the site. I helped him as well as I could, using the same technique. We hadn't got the strength to stand up.

"You were in good form", I said to Peter.

He was visibly pleased with himself and now felt certain that he had the strength to reach the summit. This was his personal altitude record, and although he was again plagued by a headache, he kept on shoving the debris to the outside of the platform. Turning to me, he said casually,

"When we climb up tomorrow, we'll only take the bare essentials with us, so that we can move even faster than today. I think I'll leave my rucksack behind."

"So will I, but I'll take the camera so long as I can carry it.

I really want to have that on the summit."

"If only I didn't have this damned headache,"

"Is it bad?"

"It always is when I reach a new height, and then just sit around."

"When we've got the tent up, I'll make you some tea. It will soon be gone."

Peter, previously so relaxed, was now tense with the pain and fearful as he looked down into the Gasherbrum Valley where the first shadows lay. His happiness had vanished without trace. He didn't

n the summit of Hidden Peak (8068m) Masherbrum in the background. This was my
ird eight thousander.

speak any more, seemed lost in thought and cold. His sudden and unusually bad headache was making him really ill.

I took out the storm tent from the rucksack, unrolled it and spread it out on the platform which we had constructed with such care. It still sloped a bit; the ice which we had laid bare by our excavations, had prevented us from levelling it out completely. Luckily we had marked the tent poles so that we had no difficulty in assembling them correctly. We slotted the aluminium A-poles together to make the front and back supports, and soon had our tiny abode erected. I was busy fixing the back of the tent and Peter sat outside near the entrance, clutching his forehead as if it might burst. "As soon as it's up properly, you can go in and lie down. If I know you, you'll be as right as rain in the morning."

We anchored the main guys of the tent with some boulders – the whole thing looked a bit cock-eyed and the walls were hanging slackly, flapping in the slightest breath of wind. Whilst Peter unpacked his rucksack to find his sleeping bag, I tried to build a kitchen in the lee of the tent.

Every fibre of my body was tired, worn out by the unbroken effort and tension of the day. Even the cooking tired me. My eyes burned from all the concentration and peering, and behind my forehead, it seemed as if a knot had formed.

BIVOUAC

It seemed to take hours before the ice melted, and almost as long again until it was warm enough to make tea. I was no longer in that halfway state between sleeping and waking, that I had been in immediately after the climb and when we put up the tent. I sipped a few mouthfuls of tea, which were just what I needed. I began to feel better and alert again. I stood up in order to stretch my legs. The fatigue gradually drained from my aching muscles and the knot of tension in my forehead disappeared.

The acute angle at which the brassy-coloured rays of the sun were striking the tent, indicated that it was already evening. I gave Peter some tea and with it he washed down his second headache tablet, then lay down again. I went on sitting on a heap of stones outside the tent, cooking, melting ice, warming soup and making more tea. While the water was simmering, I collected together the various items of equipment that were lying about and put them into some sort of order so that they could be either put on or packed without difficulty the next morning. After a while, I took some deep breaths to mobilise my strength, got up and walked a few steps to the edge of the stone patch. There was no snow, just ice. I picked up a few lumps and put them outside the tent door, so that they would be ready to hand during the evening and next morning, allowing us to cook whilst still lying in the tent.

During all these rituals, Peter lay motionless. He had forgotten we were camping high on Hidden Peak and that tomorrow was the big day. When his headache eventually began to subside, he felt as if a great weight had lifted from him. Suddenly he was filled with a pleasurable anticipation for the next day and began to concentrate entirely on getting ready for it. He worked out which clothes he would wear and the sequence in which he proposed doing things. Questions of energy conservation and tactical procedure banished everything else from his mind. He had not slept, but he had rested, and now that his head was clear again, the unbearable pressure lifted, he felt fine. He crawled out of the tent, sat next to me on the stones and began to

179

rummage in his rucksack. Nothing was missing. He got out everything he wanted for the summit attempt and deliberated again in what order they should be put on or into which pocket they should go. These negotiations occupied his whole concentration. He was like a slalom skier who must memorise his route and his whole sequence of movements before a big race, and to be absolutely sure he had it right, he went over it all again from the beginning. His back bent, his arm leaning on his rucksack, his legs out in front of him, Peter sat on the stones. He took up the aluminium pot in which I had heated the water again, poured some into a plastic beaker, but forgot to drink it. Without looking at anything in particular, he gazed out at the evening.

"What time do you think we ought to start?" he said at last.

"When the sun comes up."

Again, Peter went over the summit procedure in detail. Although he had no experience of such heights, his general climbing instincts and his knowledge, were sufficient for him to know exactly what to expect. All his decisions had been right up till now, and there was no reason why on this last critical section, his further decisions should not also be right. Everything now depended upon neither of us getting ill, and the weather staying fine, and on us being able to move fast enough to reach the summit in the early afternoon. We had mutually agreed that if we had not got there by 3 p.m., we must turn back. It would be imprudent and irresponsible to go on if we were not maintaining our expected rate of progress. The descent had to be allowed for, also. I knew from experience that a retreat from an eight-thousander in the dark, when one's strength and concentration have gone, as is inevitable at such altitudes, always spells great danger.

Peter was in a happy frame of mind all evening, if a bit quiet. He didn't eat much but drank as much as he could. He kept staring out into space. I did not try to launch any conversation, and to take my mind off the climb, I watched the sun go down behind Gasherbrum IV. We did not feel the cold until the sun's last rays had disappeared. The sky in the west was still tinged with red, and the mountains which in the morning were so clear that their every detail could be seen, now lay swimming behind a veil of mist. A little patch of light clung to the summit of Hidden Peak as I pushed my way, fully clothed, into the tent. Breathing with difficulty, I crawled into my sleeping bag, loosened my inner boots, put a second pair of gloves under my pillow, shoved the down jacket, a hat and the rucksack to the back and pressed myself to one side of the tent to leave room for Peter.

Our little stone patch was not the ideal spot for a bivouac. It was steep and exposed to the wind, but we could move outside unroped and without danger of falling, and that was important. Stretched out,

180

we lay in our sleeping bags, I to the mountain wall, Peter on the valley side. We had each shoved some clothing under our sleeping mat to try to keep it level and to prevent ourselves from rolling on top of each other in the night. I was worried by the fact that I had only been able to use one ice piton when pitching the tent; all the other guy lines were secured by loose stones. It hadn't been possible to do any more, but I couldn't shake the uneasy feeling from my head, that if there was a bad storm, we and the tent would be carried away.

Just before I began to do the last cooking that evening, the first stars appeared in the darkening sky. Night comes a little later up here than it does in the valleys. We had no idea, of course, what the weather forecast was, but I felt pretty sure that the next day would be fine. I kept brewing up tea on the little gas stove, which was very wobbly, although I had tried to balance it on a flat stone in the tent entrance. The water boiled but didn't really get hot. We were pressed in so close to each other that neither of us could make the slightest movement without disturbing the other. Peter lay half on his back with his face to the side of the tent, I on my stomach. Now and then I would fiddle with the cooker which was hissing intermittently; up here in the oxygen-starved air, the stove didn't make its accustomed buzzing sound, but an almost inaudible hum, at times so indistinct that I had to look to make sure the flame had not gone out.

By turns, we drank tea, silently and without really enjoying it. We drank simply because we had to. During the late afternoon we had had a few bites of dried plums and bread, but we had not the slightest desire for a big meal. We had a stale, sticky taste in our dehydrated mouths, which the tea only relieved for a few seconds. The warm drinks helped against the thirst and to keep us warm. This brew-up lasted more than an hour, and at times we alternated the tea with a mug of soup.

Lying in the bivouac with nothing to do, I tried to go over the events of the day to take my mind off other thoughts, but without success. Peter was lying there with his mouth open. From his movements, I guessed he was awake too. Hoar frost had collected an inch thick on the tent walls. When Peter did go to sleep, his breath rattled in his throat due to the lack of oxygen.

Scraps of verse ran through my head "... with the Gods, thou shalt not compete... with the Gods..." I didn't know the next bit, then, "He must pass along this empty road..." Strange disjointed snatches; like telegrams, these fragments arrived in my head; it was like learning something parrot-fashion at school.

"Man must be free to bring something to a peaceful end; free from women, free from desire, free from fear." At last a complete sentence.

181

I wondered what the time was – 3 o'clock perhaps, or 4. It was still quite dark inside the tent, clear and starry outside.

IN THE DEATH ZONE

"We'll rest above the 'Sickle'." The hollow that from the Gasherbrum Valley looks like a recumbent sickle, was in reality a great concave basin, steep and icy. On a tiny platform that Peter had trodden in the snow, we rested for the first time since our start at 8 o'clock that morning. From the ridge we could see far below the yellow tent where we had passed the night. The little stone patch now lay in the sunshine. It occurred to me that there was nobody – neither at Base Camp, nor at home – who knew where we were at this hour. It didn't bother me at all. On the contrary, I was quite glad. We were in every respect inaccessible. Nobody could get to us, even in an emergency.

The next rest was on a rock block, 28 steps further on. Then we climbed through the basin – technically easy, but strenuous. I again counted the steps: nine, ten, eleven. . . . twenty-four, twenty-five. It grew steeper further up; this I had noticed from photographs. We were aiming for the area where the North and North-west Faces come together. After every twenty-five or twenty-eight steps we were as worn out as if we had just run a race, and there were something like another 200 of these stretches to do before we reached the summit. It was a good thing we had started when we did. We were still fairly low down, but that didn't matter. We were on our way. The goal we still knew only in imagination, but it was a goal. Willpower can carry a belief into success.

Another 25 steps. We couldn't see much, just the toes of our boots in the snow, and our hands. Each step was a repetition of the last – twenty-one, twenty-two. . . . When we had a chance to sit down, we looked back down to the valley. What a view! Magnificent! Peaks as far as the eye could see, fading away to the horizon. We were far above the mist.

200 metres further up, I had to take off my right boot. I could not feel my toes any more. Awkward manoeuvre: gaiters off, outer boots, stocking, innerboot, felt boot, more socks. Carefully I massaged the stumps of my amputated toes. If anyone could have seen us up there, muffled to the eyebrows, ponderous in our movements, he would

scarcely have taken us for human beings.

Once we reached the ridge, separating the two faces, North and Northwest, we stopped for a while. To the left it was steep and rocky and obviously too dangerous. So we passed to the right. The valleys and gorges were now filled with sunlight. In the distance the mountains were partly obscured by mist. Now and then Peter would say "It's going OK" or "That's Tibet over there!"

"Yes" I would answer.

The importance of these sentences lay more in their utterance than in their content. We wanted to reassure ourselves that we were bearing up all right and still capable of thinking straight.

For a while we had been climbing up an S-shaped gully, but it was becoming very strenuous and likely to avalanche; there was too much fresh snow. We left the gully and climbed the rock ribs instead. We were visibly gaining height. We could now see K2. In the distance were white clouds on the horizon, single small clouds like pearly fishes.

When, after two dozen steps, I took my regular breather, leaning into the slope, clasping my axe, the shaft of which I had firmly driven into the snow before my strength ran out, I could feel my heart thundering away. I could feel it from my calves to the crown of my head. Slowly the pounding died down and again I heard the gentle singing, the strange almost monotonous sound I had encountered the day before. A regular sound that came from the snow and the rock. It was not the wind. Probably Peter heard it as strongly as I. At the end of our rest breaks, it was at its clearest. Not a human voice. A singing that was there only when both of us were still.

We were lucky with the weather. It remained fine like the day before. Straddling a rocky gully, Peter's right crampon had worked loose. His red gaiters, which enveloped his whole foot from bootsole to knee, were getting in his way as he climbed. He was having trouble tightening the strap of his crampons. He took the gaiter off, and set it down on a rock with a stone upon it.

We were standing in the middle of the ice wilderness that was the summit wall. Looking up, everything seemed peaceful; thin snow plumes hung motionless over the corniced ridge. There was not a breath of wind, although the air was light and cold. The snow surface undisturbed and trackless, as it had been for thousands of years. The voice of the mountain had sunk to a dreamy humming, which would stop completely now and again, and then start up again.

Peter was only doing what was absolutely essential. Probably to husband his strength, he was climbing straight upwards. Now he had reached a narrow rock rib above me and stared down. Mechanically he adjusted his crampon again. I was as concerned for Peter's health and safety, as for my own. Not in the way that a guide takes care of his client, but a much more personal involvement. All the time I thought of us as a single unit. Although we were not roped together, we felt like a roped party. We were a self-created entity. There was something synchronous about the way we thought, the way we did things. A short glance was enough to ascertain the other's intention and frame of mind, to know and do what the other wanted. It wasn't just shared exploits in the past that gave us this heightened mutual understanding; it was also the extreme tension we were sharing now. And our feeling of one-ness grew, along with our concentration, the nearer we drew to the summit. Peter kept saying the same thing that I had thought a moment before. But it was not even necessary to speak to feel the communication flow between us. Even 20 or 40 paces apart, the one senses what the other did, saw or thought. And always the one climbing ahead had the responsibility for finding the best passage, the second following unconditionally, behind. The change of lead, whilst not precise, took place around every 200 metres.

I had been conscious of Peter's determination all day – he seemed to know that we would get to the summit and back to the bivouac without trouble. All yesterday's hesitations and uncertainties had vanished and a deep peace began to pervade our senses.

We were more conscious of the altitude towards the end of the morning and were forced to rest more often. Peter, who was again in the lead, was not just stamping his way up the hard firn, but taking the trouble to cut little regular steps. Suddenly he interrupted the usual silence of a rest pause by asking:

"How's it going then, Reinhold?"

I raised myself from my axe and turning to him, grinned optimistically, "We're going fast enough", I said, "We should do it all right." Then I gasped again, sunk on my axe, as always during these breathers. Before I began climbing again, I exchanged a glance with Peter. I was just about to climb past him when he said, "Up there, that must be the ridge, the summit ridge."

Fine snow crystals floated between us and the deep blue sky, sparkling, evanescent. The snow dust hung in the air with a peculiar weightlessness, the effect accentuated by there being absolutely no wind, nor a cloud to be seen from far or near. For the first time I was climbing the summit of an eight-thousander in perfect calm, no atmosphere disturbances at all. Even the sun was relatively warm, and not once did my breath freeze in my beard. Neither of us spoke. The vault of the sky and the glassy air reminded me of a flight I once made from Djakarta to Singapore. The gradient of the wall began to ease off; the higher we climbed, the less it became.

Peter Habeler at 7200m   ... at 7500m   ... at 7800m.

At a great altitude, when no oxygen is used, it only takes a few hours for the facial appearance of a climber to alter considerably. Movement, will power and lucidity are also affected. In three hours - 600m difference in height, Peter Habeler looked ten years older.

At first softly, then by degrees becoming louder, we heard a roaring above our heads, a roaring like giant bellows at work. As Peter reached the ridge, the sun and the wind caught his hair. Below, where I was, the air was still calm. I stamped upwards, hoping to film his further progress. Convinced now, that we would soon be there, Peter said only,

"This is the summit ridge."

Then he pulled his axe out of the snow and went on climbing. The wind was very strong up here, but not unpleasant. It absorbed the sound of my laboured breathing and my heavy steps in the snow.

We arrived at the ridge between the Northwest Face and the Southwest Flank and, looking over the Eastern Summit of Hidden Peak, were treated to a stupendous panorama of Tibet, which surpassed anything I had ever seen before. A mountain landscape in grey and white, fanning out from crest to crest into eternity, ridges like the petrified waves of a gigantic sea. To the left the highest peaks in the Karakorum – three eight-thousanders – Gasherbrum II, Broad Peak, K2 – the frontier mountains between Tibet and Pakistan. Their irrational thrust into the blue-black sky staggers the mind, heightens the sense of loftiness and isolation.

The isolation was, in fact, overwhelming. When I thought about it, how long it had taken us to get this far, it seemed we had reached eternity. It was as still and quiet as Space. I have always sought solitude. For many years I have been developing the independence to withstand it, and now at last I have found the inner peace to survive it.

Up here, close to the summit, the world stands still in time. The raging of the wind and the humming from the heart of the mountain blanket off the life of the valleys. These surging sounds and the changing colours of the serrated scene, come together on our summit, come together in black and white. The atmosphere was impregnated with silence, not the infinite silence of death, but the liberating silence of infinity, light and carefree. All sounds were like deep silence, each movement was neither work nor action, merely being. And being was freedom. And freedom was older than time.

In the viewfinder of my camera I could hardly make out Peter at all. His dark figure merged with the black background of the sky. Only when he moved a few steps could I see his feet in the snow. He was now standing on the highest cornice, dissolving into nothingness. I could not tell how far away he was.

The thought of at last reaching the summit after this demanding climb, overcame all his tiredness, and I noticed how he consciously quickened his pace with a sense of triumph. He did not fully register that he was on the top until he could look down the west side of the mountain to the Abruzzi Glacier, and to make quite sure, he crossed to the other side, going down to the first rocks. Here he put in the single piton we had brought with us to the summit. As he turned back onto the snow dome, we met and embraced. Peter could barely restrain his tears of joy. We sat there a long time in silence, gazing all around. The spontaneous exhilaration gave way to tranquillity. The sounds of silence began again. A drowsiness overcame us, permeating all our thoughts, sights and feelings. Only the tracks in the hard snow, and the iceaxe bearing the tiny European flag, reminded us that we sat on the highest point of Hidden Peak. The sky over the mountain was spun with a fine web-like tracery, flecked with purple and gold. The mountains themselves – Baltoro Kangri, Chogolisa, Masherbrum, Mustagh Tower, the Gasherbrums, Broad Peak, K2 – presented a chaos of angled flanks and walls, here and there barring the distant view. Behind them darker ranges merged with the sky. Above, like white minarets, hung the clouds.

We sat at the apex of endless space. Far below in the valleys lay a milky mist. The horizon around spread like the emptiness within. With serene unconcern, I awoke from my state of bliss, from a kind of Nirvana.

We must start down again, back to the bivouac.

Facing the wall, we each made our way down our old tracks. All

plans and thoughts no longer directed towards the summit, but of Base Camp, and beyond that, home. Fresh thoughts had entered my sub-conscious:

"We did it" ... "My third eight-thousander" ... "The first man to climb three eight-thousanders."

We rested less often, tiredness and time were forgotten. In less than two hours we were 100 metres above 'the Sickle' and it was beginning to level out. I forced myself on, step in front of step.

In the clear light of late afternoon we stumbled to the tent, which we had been able to see from a long way off. The evening meal consisted of soup, tea and chocolate. We lay down in the tent, listening to the sounds of the evening and enjoying the sunset. Finally, we took off our heavy outer boots and crawled into our sleeping bags. I slept well, but in the first grey light of dawn, I found myself counting "fifteen...six-teen...seventeen", over and over senselessly, counting the steps.

Peter started awake from his light sleep, struggling to draw breath like someone who has been shut up in a plastic bag. The strong wind and the flapping of the tent walls built an acoustic bridge between the narrow tent and the cold night outside. Peter opened and shut his eyes a couple of times, blinking in the dawn twilight, trying to place him-self. It was around 5 o'clock in the morning.

Now I could see that the tent had torn at the front end. The wind was blowing fine powder snow into the opening, and it was quickly piling up inside. One of us in his sleep must have kicked too violently against the equipment stowed at the end of the tent, and the gale had torn it. Peter had gone back to sleep and this dramatically altered situation, serious as it was, failed to rouse him. As the weight of the snow built up on his legs, he merely jerked his feet convulsively towards him. To escape from the icy snow which kept blowing round my face, I pulled my down jacket over my head. My movements were clumsy, almost automatic, like someone pulling up the bedclothes in his sleep but the wind blew so icily through the tent that I couldn't stand it any more and I sat up to see what I could do about it. My hair and pullover were covered in snow and, at the foot of the tent, more and more snow was swirling in. The inside of the tent differed very little from the outside, tempestuous and uncomfortable. We could only attribute it to our tiredness, that we had slept in so late, but the situation was now so drastic there could be no more sleep.

The wind was whistling over all the ridges with a roaring and moaning that drowned out our voices and the fluttering of the tent. It blew with such violence that I feared we could not withstand it; together with the tent, we would simply be carried away.

I opened the tent door and for a moment had the feeling of receiving the full blast from a forge-bellows. Instinctively, Peter and I grabbed up all the loose odds and ends and stuffed everything we were not going to wear into our rucksacks. We took out our sleeping bags and tried to roll them up in the howling wind. We wanted to leave the campsite as soon as possible. As we put on our boots, some of our clothes began flying about, and we looked up quickly to check that our crampons and axes were still there. We sat on our rucksacks and watched the storm ripping the tent to shreds. Now that it was empty and light, it billowed out, straining on its guy lines like a parachute. The lumps of rock we had used to anchor it down had frozen into the ice and held, but some of the guys had snapped and now a loose corner of the tent was flapping so wildly it made a whip-cracking noise.

Although we were still tired and numb from the cold, we had to start down right away. We knew that the longer we stayed up here, the more difficult the descent would become, and the earlier we got back to the valley, the better for us. Again we took only the bare essentials with us and left everything else behind – gas cooker, spare food, the climbing gear we wouldn't be needing in the next few days. In a very short while these things would have either blown away in the wind, or frozen into the ice. As we were tying our sleeping mats to our rucksacks, a gust of wind blew the tent over.

"We were lucky that we were already dressed", said Peter.

Although the tension that had accompanied us step by step during the ascent had now evaporated, we had still to put our full concentration into the task of getting down. We knew that a descent requires every bit as much care as coming up. In the conditions that now faced us, the descent was in fact far more difficult than the climb itself.

If we wanted to survive the first 1,000 metres, we must put every last ounce of energy and skill into the task. Whatever it cost, we must reach the Gasherbrum Valley in one piece. Further down we could crawl out on our hands and knees, if necessary.

Satisfaction at having been the first two-man expedition to climb an eight-thousander, had receded now, far into the background. The actuality of the difficult descent was the prime consideration. We were still sitting on the edge of our stone terrace, now lit by the first grey light of day; the surrounding peaks were flushed with rose, while in the valleys, it was still night. There was no storm down there. Peter and I were still wearing the same clothing as when we came up, we each now carried our rucksacks. We had with us our cameras, the cine-camera and the exposed film, and the necessary food. We began our descent, treading uncertainly the few steps to the edge of the plateau, the wind behind us, trying to blow us over.

The face fell away at an alarming angle. It took a good deal of courage to step off the firm ground down into the seemingly-endless abyss. But get down we must. The wind was not so fierce on the face as it had been up at the bivouac. Even up there, it didn't seem to rage as loudly as before. Perhaps when the sun came up, it would cease altogether. A stone broke away under my crampon, and went crashing down the face. It sounded uncommonly loud, for a moment drowning out the sound of the storm over our heads. Peter turned to watch it go, with each bound setting off small avalanches. From the speed of the falling stones and the distance they fell, some indication of the steepness and sweep of the face could be estimated. Peter's caution and resolve did not wilt in the face of this disconcerting knowledge. Before long having recovered our composure and rhythm, we were climbing down by the same route as we had come up. Facing into the mountain, we would take a few steps whilst we carefully held onto the rocks with our hands, then, with our feet securely placed, we felt for more handholds lower down, automatically following the three-points-of-contact rule. Then Peter climbed into a chimney directly below me and I was able to watch his progress through my legs. We hadn't had time before we set off to talk over a plan of campaign, so now and then we exchanged a few words:

"It's nothing like as bad as I feared", said Peter.

"No", I muttered.

He continued to climb down, as if in a trance. When he reached a safe stance, he would stop and let me lead through, so that he could take it more easily at the back. When I was out in front, I was careful to deviate slightly from the fall-line of our ascent route, to keep out of the way of possibly loosened stones. This was not always possible, and certainly not when we were obliged to follow narrow gullies, sometimes descending one immediately below the other. Any little stone knocked off by the top man could have knocked the lower one off the face. We therefore took great care to keep the distance between us as narrow as possible, and not to let our concentration wander, although we were so tired.

"Watch out! Stones!"

I looked up at Peter and saw he had dislodged something that was coming straight for me. I dodged it and watched it hurtling down into the depths.

"Did it hit you?" cried Peter in an alarmed voice.

I held my breath unwittingly for the space of a heartbeat, before answering "No."

Peter studied the rocks on which he stood and moved to the right to reach a gully that promised to be less dangerous. We made vexatiously slow progress to start with. The snow was sometimes floury, so that the crampons scratched the rock, and sometimes so hard that the crampons wouldn't bite into it at all. We had to place each step very precisely for fear that the snow would suddenly break away or the foot slip off the surface. Even the gullies at an angle of about 60° were full of snow because they narrowed lower down like bottlenecks. In contrast to climbing up, we could now take many more steps without having to rest, and when we did pause, we no longer simply stopped in our tracks, but took care to cut a level stance so that we could stand comfortably. Basically, this was not a complicated descent, but neither was it monotonous. It cost a lot of energy although with each step we were moving down into less rarefied air.

I kept coming back to the conclusion that to employ belaying tactics, as we would have liked, didn't in fact make a lot of sense. We could not have always found or prepared a suitable belay stance. Precautions are only possible on this kind of wall, if the climber can carry sufficient pegs to make his own belays.

The last third of the descent was the most strenuous and therefore the most dangerous. The face here was steep and at times, completely blank, so that one could only get the frontmost points of the 12-pointer crampons into its surface. We maintained our balance with an axe in

191

We descended the way we had come up, step by step, facing inwards.

the right hand and a peg in the left, and pausing to rest more often. Although we were not belaying, we relied on each other for psychological support. The slightest slip of the foot would have inevitably resulted in a fall, and though the face flattened out below, no-one could have survived a fall into the Gasherbrum Valley. So we climbed on with great caution and didn't let our minds dwell on the possible outcome of a moment's carelessness. Although we were making quite good time, it felt to us as if we went at a snail's pace. At each stop I calculated the distance we still had to go to reach the foot of the wall.

"Be careful to cut big enough steps in the ice, so that you can rest properly," was the good advice I gave myself, and "Don't let your rucksack upset your balance."

In four hours we had made about 600 metres; it was about as much again to the Bergschrund, which we could now see as a narrow black line far below. Peter was panting from fatigue. The face was still in the shade and the icy air was affecting his lungs. His arms seemed as heavy as lead from the constant weight of the peg and axe, and his legs were in danger of giving out. If he stopped for a few minutes to rest, he merely exchanged one torment for another. The enfeebling heaviness of his legs and the pain in his lungs receded, but his muscles would be seized with cramp. He groaned from weariness. Flecks of sweat and spittle were frozen into his beard and moustache.

The Gasherbrum Valley was still discouragingly far away and it was better not to think too seriously about it, but to concentrate on the immediate prospect, the sheer endless ice slope under our feet. More steps, more blows in the hard ice to fashion a notch to stand up in. Five hours we had spent already and still had 300 metres more to the foot of the face. Our rest pauses became more frequent and lasted longer and longer. I tried all manner of tricks to make the distance between each stop greater. By telling myself that once down all my troubles would be over, I extracted the last ounce out of myself. "Just one more step, then you can rest again" I would say, and I kept repeating this 'just one more step' thereby managing to lengthen the climbing stretches between pauses.

Out of the corner of my eye, I suddenly saw that Peter, who was climbing directly underneath me, had thrown off his rucksack. In crazy leaps and bounds, it bounced down the face and rolled into the Gasherbrum Valley below. At this spectacle, a cold shudder ran through me, before I realised that he had kept his balance despite the sudden loss of weight, and was watching the progress of his rucksack with equanimity. His right crampon had obviously worked loose again and in order to refasten it, he had had to remove his sack. With such an awkward load on his back, he had not enough manoeuvring room to tighten the straps.

This made me realise that my own crampons were loose. I hesitated a moment, then without thinking any more about it, I took the strap of my own rucksack off my shoulder, turned slightly, and got rid of my load too. Like Peter's a few moments earlier, my rucksack also whistled down the face. The red bundle first rolled, then made great bounds, before sailing over the bergschrund and dashing itself into the snow. It didn't matter to me whether I found all the bits and pieces again or not. The most important thing at that moment was that the crampons should be securely fixed and that I didn't myself go headlong down the wall after my sack. My thoughts were still with the two rucksacks as I resumed my own descent. Suddenly there was a creaking sound under my foot and I noticed a large lump of ice, part of the crust, break away and begin to slide. Immediately I took my weight onto my arms, just in the nick of time; a couple of steps with my feet and I was secure again. The ice whizzed down the slope and was soon scattered in a thousand tiny fragments. Instinctively, I now tried to distribute my weight equally between my arms and legs, and so allow myself a greater area of balance; and to avert the constant danger of another slip I now climbed with my axe and piton. During the halts I thought of nothing in particular. Peter was crouching on a relatively comfortable platform and adjusting his crampons again. His eyes were fixed, and the snow which clung to his clothing, gave him the appearance of being a rock in the middle of the blank ice slope.

An hour later we reached the Gasherbrum Valley and recovered our rucksacks. Were we thirsty! My tongue clove to the roof of my mouth like a piece of old leather, and my throat was caked with dust. We had drunk nothing since the previous evening and parched, we struggled down to the bivouac site where we had left a gas cooker and some full cartridges.

The sky was the colour of water on mossy stones. Far away in the valley lay a small lake. No, that wasn't a lake, it was a crevasse; the long, dark shape to the right of our first campsite was a crevasse. What was the matter with me, going crazy or simply plagued with hallucinations?

Peter went on ahead. He no longer walked like a man, but an automaton, his will was his motor. He was on the brink of collapse but his feet kept going. Bent forwards and taking tiny, even steps, he just went on, and on, and on. Had he fallen, he would never have got up again.

After a four hour rest at the bivouac place, we pulled ourselves together, packed such things as we thought we would immediately need, and began the descent of the icefall in direction of Base Camp. But we didn't get far. The snow was soft, the sun's fire unendurable. After 200 metres – Peter having just stepped into his second crevasse – we decided to turn back to the bivouac and go down the following morning.

The evening and night passed in a flash. Slowly the weariness ebbed from our dehydrated bodies. Towards morning, the wind had almost died away: instead of the fluttering of the tent, we just heard a dreamy singing. The unaccustomed silence made me sleepy and confused. For a while I just dozed, hearing again in my dreams, the howling of the storm the previous night, and imagining the tent tearing to pieces once more. It was, it seemed to me, like coming to the end of a night journey in an open wagon. Fine snow dust forced its way through the ventilation holes of the bivouac tent.

As Peter and I crawled out of the bivouac the next morning, the snow that had gathered on our sleeping bags during the night, crumbled onto our insulating mats. Peter struggled to his feet and tried, unsuccessfully, to straighten up. He looked around – rocks, mountains, a patch of sky and in the south, the summit wall of Hidden Peak which now barred the view towards Tibet. The heavens had that blue-white colour that heralds a settled period of fine weather, the eastern horizon was flushed with gold. The blue in the valleys was semi-transparent, the snow in the morning light, a dusty grey.

The descent to Base Camp on that morning of August 12th was like a pleasant stroll – rucksacks half empty, snow hard, glacier bridges frozen, we ambled along. Both of the icefalls had changed considerably, but we found our way without any trouble. The Polish climbers, who were not away in a high camp with their leader, Wanda Rutkiewicz, were the first to congratulate us. They kept speaking of a new epoch in alpinism that we had introduced, and a new, logical approach that we had demonstrated to adventurers of the younger generation. We were, they said, the first to apply a sporting concept to hard Himalayan climbing, to the last bastions unspoiled by technical development.

We ourselves had been less inspired by such thoughts as by a fascination for one of the hardest wildernesses in the world, and with the question of the survival potential of two men alone in such a critical situation. This expedition had not only showed me that an eight-thousander can be climbed by two exactly in the same way as an alpine peak, but it had also given me an answer to the question of mankind's fundamental existence. Already, I had begun to see myself in a new relationship with the world.

Sometimes I asked myself what would have happened if we had perished on the summit of Hidden Peak, or if we hadn't even got that far. It would have made no difference to the world. Only Peter and I would have ceased to be.

On July 13th we had left Skardu bound for Base Camp; on August 13th, together with Khaled, we left Base Camp for the march back to Skardu. We had been able to acclimatise for four weeks and had taken five days on the actual climb. We had preceded the Graz group to the summit of Hidden Peak by one day – even though they had started out two weeks before us, and had used oxygen and equipped high camps for the final assault. Was our system therefore better? No, there is no better or worse, our system was different, that's all. Schell and his party had followed typical expedition procedure and could be well satisfied that they had been one of the smallest expeditions ever to reach an eight-thousand metre summit.

On the second day of the return march, on the way from Concordia to Urdukas, the heavens opened without warning, subjecting us to torrents of icy rain. It was impossible to predict how long it might last. It was wet and murky. A brew of mist, lashing rain, hail and snow was directed into our faces by the wind. Like tiny needles the hailstones stabbed our skin, stinging our faces. Water ran from our hair, down our backs and into our boots. Our feet were numb with cold. To this was added raging streams, wet stones and the persistent, deafening roar of water and the howling of the wind. Off and on, in the distance, we could hear the rumbling of avalanches coming down to left and right of the glacier. Frequently we missed our way and had to pick our steps back through the crevasses and seek another route. The storm continued for another half an hour after we had reached Urdukas, then suddenly everything was perfectly calm again. As the grass and stones were shining fresh after the deluge, so my thoughts too became clear as the discomfort passed.

Wtih the water bottle in my hand I prepared to go off and look for a spring when I was aware of a squelching sound; no wonder my feet were icy cold, the water in my boots came as high as my ankles. I must first change my clothes. Meanwhile, the spring from which we had drunk on the way-in had run dry. I looked further afield until a rhythmic plopping amongst the stones indicated I was on the right track. With difficulty I found the underground spring, which though small, gave a steady trickle of water. In 20 minutes I had filled my flask.

The next morning, nearing Liligo, we came to a milky-grey glacier beck barring our progress. Unlike on the march-in, I no longer asked "How will we get across?" We simply crossed it. The uncertainty that dogs the start of a venture and is so hard to dispel, was no longer a problem. With every day and every step put behind us, we became more and more determined. Obstacles were no longer obstacles; they were merely things to overcome. It required no exercise of will for we no longer feared trouble or danger. We had no qualms about crossing the river, although had we met it on the march-in, we should probably have waited a whole night until the water-level went down. From where did this resolve suddenly come? Why were we prepared to be so much harsher with ourselves? Maybe we had learnt to withstand hunger and hardship more easily, and we no longer needed to shepherd our strength, spare our skin. We were ruthless with ourselves, and took on each new difficulty without a thought. I stumbled out into the middle of the river, my legs numb in the icy waters. I didn't hesitate until the water came up to my waist, only then did I stop. The stones were crashing against my legs and each blow shoved me a little further downstream, but I felt no pain although I was black and blue afterwards. Peter followed me; we held on to each other to keep our balance. When we were in the middle of the river struggling, our minds had already reached the other side. With our eyes firmly fixed on the far bank, we held our breath and plunged into the deepest eddies; the water tugged at us but it didn't move us, so strong was our resolve.

Day by day, we lengthened the stages we trekked along the pitiless Baltoro Glacier. "We've only got to do it once" we would say to ourselves. We moved completely automatically, our lips cracked, the skin peeling from our noses and cheeks. 50 kilometres in ten hours. We stayed two days in Askole, the first village – meadows, trees, people! The sounds of the early morning were music to our ears – the chirping of the crickets and cicadas, the birdsong. Somewhere a cock crowed and off and on a dog barked. We heard the peasants leading oxen to the fields, children chattering, young girls singing. Nevertheless, we wanted to go on. More endless desert.

"Were we ever there?" Peter had trouble remembering some of the episodes. The loss of memory, common after an ascent of this altitude, became evident. I recalled something Uschi had once said to a reporter who was curious to know what happened to the human faculties at

196

extreme altitude. She answered,

"Reinhold keeps on going till he doesn't even recognise his own wife any more."

Uschi. I wondered how she was getting on.

When I had been away on Lhotse, it hadn't been too bad for her. She had hardly worried because she knew the team was experienced and that in a few weeks she would be with us, perhaps even in time for the summit bid. This time it was quite different. Uschi was completely detached from what was happening to us. She was anxious and tired. She brooded over every detail. I believe it is all a question of inner harmony. If a person feels part of his surroundings, part of a circle of friends, it is easy to be gay and even-tempered. Basically, Uschi is a person who doesn't mind being alone, but lately she had become very wrapped up with me and my activities. Now she felt deserted as well as lonely. By a chain of adverse circumstances, she had been thrown out of kilter, and could not bear the isolation.

During the return march I kept my thoughts on Uschi. She was a palpable vision before me. I saw her every day as I trudged along, and at nights she appeared to me when I was half-asleep between those nightmares that always bothered me on my way back to civilisation after a big expedition.

For half an hour in Chongo, among the branches of the first apricot trees, I forgot everything. The sheer delight of the physical exercise flowed through my limbs. It was as if my whole body had grown lighter and at the same time, stronger.

"I could go on like this for years, on and on forever."

The cultivated terraces in the valley looked marshy this morning; there were puddles and waterholes everywhere, glistening in the sun. They contrasted strikingly with the parched brown mountainsides above, rising straight out of the valley floor. Despite the early hour, the sun was already high, the air over the fields pleasant and almost cool. It stirred a memory of spring within me – spring in the South Tyrol. A day in April more than twenty years ago, with flowers on the meadows, little streams, moist earth and fresh greenery. A time that belonged to the few really happy weeks of my life.

How many years was it since I had spent a spring at home? Six, or seven? Spring is different, and comes at different times, all over the world. But at home it is softer. The meadows are like carpets and the air as clear as spring water. Here the earth was warm and damp too but less young. I took my boots off. "Next spring I'll stay at home" said I, inspired by my bare feet.

It was still early morning when we left Chongo. The sound of tumbling water mingled with the sound of the wind became a rising and falling symphony to accompany us on our way. We took off our shirts and walked bare-chested through the fields, along the bush-lined irrigation channels. The dewy foliage caressed my arms and breast, the water droplets clung like blossoms to my skin.

How thin my arms had become. These arms that had pulled me up onto the narrowest of ledges, looked now like the wasted arms of any unfit office worker. I weighed only 59 kilogrammes, I had lost 16 pounds.

"The scree traverse shouldn't be a problem this time."

A glance at the slopes brought back memories of the march-in, the laden porters, spilt blood, a rolling body, Khaled like a living stone in the water, terrified men sucked under and reappearing, a dropped load floating away. Five weeks ago the stones had fallen everywhere for a distance of 10, 20, 30 metres. Nothing but stones. Stones like missiles, and with them, mud. This time too, the stones were whistling about our heads. Again we had to duck, take cover. The stone avalanche had barely finished when I looked up. Peter was running as the last fragments splashed into the water. We must get out of this vicious gorge before the next load came down, before it was too late. We were right in the middle of the traverse, no time to dither. I firmly clutched the arm of a porter we had hired in Askole, and at a signal from Peter, came on. A few hasty steps, a pause to recover balance, and on. Our feet scarcely disturbed the slope. If a hold broke away, I was usually already past it on my way to the next sheltered spot. We came to another ravaged gully, another narrow track in the soft conglomerate, down which the stones coursed. The porter behind me hesitated. This was no place to stop and think; I shouted at him "Go!"

We hadn't a second to lose. The pauses between the volleys were very short. There was no escape and we hurried on to get to the end of the dangerous passage. Another 500, another 400 metres. We kept on scrambling along the side of the Braldo, often as much as 50 metres above the river. The treacherous scree above gave us no peace; every instant the slope would dance into life and there was no telling from where the stones would come next. From a height of 500 metres a number would hurtle down the mountainside together, each stone bringing a second with it, so that by the time they reached us, there would be hundreds of them, stones as large as a man's fist. They bounded over the vertical steps, whistled through the air and crashed down in a thousand pieces.

Every few minutes we rested under overhangs and projections. But it wasn't possible to be safe even there. The whole mountainside seemed ready to fall. Our porter was cowering down, shivering to the very roots of his hair, and we still had at least 100 metres to go before we were out of the danger zone. Suddenly the bank gave way under my feet, the river had undermined it. I realised what was happening and quick as lightning, jumped down onto a projecting boulder. The water washed around my feet, then, as the slice of earth, as big as a room, came down and hit the river behind me, the water closed over my head. I surfaced and spluttered, looking first at the porter, then at Peter, who was behaving as if nothing had happened.

"Everything okay?"

"Sahib soaked – hopefully comes nothing from above – hopefully not now", said the scared porter.

"It's a bastard, this traverse", commented Peter and gave the sign for the porter to go on. "Hurry, hurry, we mustn't hang about here!" Then as an encouragement to me, he added "Long live the crow!"

The porter was still wavering under his overhang, crouched down as if in a bunker. The nature of the wall varied every inch of the way, sometimes it was earthy, sometimes scree, sometimes humpy vertical rock. Now and then I scratched a few steps in the muddy scree with my axe, an inducement for the porter to follow.

After the last passages with our lives in peril, my tiredness had increased a hundred fold. How far was it now to Dassu? Days or hours? I had no further conception of time, and had given up trying to gauge it any more.

DRIFTING DOWN THE BRALDO

We looked now like a pair of desert foxes, no longer like 'Romeo and Juliet', as one good friend had dubbed us when we set off from Munich. Romeo and Juliet on safari! That made even Peter laugh. And yet the comparison was not totally absurd. We did have this peculiar synchronisation of responses, even during the march-out. It wasn't that we were particularly fond of each other and we didn't speak very much, but either one of us would have given his life to save the other.

Every man has only a certain amount of energy at his disposal. Once this is exhausted, he loses his will to struggle against death. Certainly he can regenerate his resources, but it takes time. From my six consecutive months spent on expeditions, I was now utterly drained, as tired as if I had just come through a serious illness. This heat and this lassitude, and the mosquitoes by night, whining like sirens round my ears, oppressed me.

In Dassu it was raining and we waited a whole afternoon and a morning for the jeep to Skardu. For four hours we travelled through the sun-scourged valleys, drawing a cloud of dust behind us. Then the hateful journey was over and we sat again in Skardu. I saw myself in the mirror for the first time in five weeks; I looked so old, I ought to have had grey hair. We had packed into 38 days the experience of a lifetime. It was too much.

I went straight away to the post office, convinced that something special would be waiting for me. There had to be something from Uschi – a letter perhaps, or even a few lines on a postcard. Even to see her name would have given me pleasure; on this day her handwriting alone would have seemed like a caress.

I refused to believe that there was nothing for me, and leafed through the bundles of letters until I found one addressed to me, but it was from the Ministry of Tourism in Islamabad granting us an extension to our permit until September 15th.

It was my turn to feel abandoned. As I stood there, weary and desolate, I wanted desperately to know how Uschi was getting on.

"Where is the Telegraph Office?"

"Round at the back, in the same building," the Postmaster answered amicably.

One chair and two small tables. The official stood outside, he didn't look as if he was very busy. It was still early morning. As I wrote out the text, I thought to myself that in two or three days. Uschi would know all about it: "Hidden Peak climbed, In Love, Reinhold."

Then Peter and I meandered through the narrow streets of Skardu without jackets and in our broken-down boots. It was hot, as hot as it had been six weeks before. The dust hung like smoke on the roofs. There was a clear blue sky and no wind. As we wandered, I saw again all the shops where I had made our purchases. Why there were no flights in this fine weather, was a mystery to us. But I now knew the rules of this game of chance. And so, the next day too, we walked the streets of the town, drinking tea and buying fruit.

And in my dreams at night, I would be floating down the Braldo. Even when half-awake, or lost in thought, stumbling through the dusty lanes, I was still under its spell. The river would carry me on to other worlds.

Two nights later, still in Skardu, in a bare cement-grey room I had another glimpse of Nirvana. I was once again in the freedom beyond the clouds, all hopes shed. There was no longer anything I needed for support; nothing in the whole world that frightened me; nothing whereafter I was consumed with desire. I simply was , that was all. And lazily floating down the Braldo.

During these hours, echoes of the events of the past few weeks relived in my consciousness – memories sometimes disconnected, sometimes muddled. Often when I awoke, I was in the middle of the face again, and once I was on the summit itself. I would gladly have stayed there forever, but reality soon overcame sensation.

We had accomplished the return journey from Base Camp to Skardu in a week – one week to cover the 70 kilometres of glacier, 70 kilometres along the Braldo banks, 60 kilometres through the desert. And the outcome of all this was that we were trapped for four days in this dusty, windy town waiting for a flight. There had been no planes to Rawalpindi for weeks. I withdrew into myself, lying there in the cheerless room, over-burdened with the impressions of the past six months, which recurred and recurred in my feverish dreams. Seen in the blue light of early morning, the valley basin around Skardu seemed desolate and forlorn. In front of the Rest House were piles of dirt, through which a nervous dog was hungrily nosing. A feeble light rising over the brown mountains broke through the clouds in the east. And below flowed the Braldo, languidly, ceaselessly.

Still not flying weather.

I must have been in a trance, for later I didn't remember getting back into bed. Again I was lying outstretched in the water, my weak and heavy limbs supported by the billows, and pictures kept floating by – Tengpoche, Camp III on Lhotse, Urdukas, Concordia, the moraine at the snout of the Baltoro, a village, a tiny oasis. . . . This interminable river kept flowing to the sea. I was alone, a bundle of experiences, drifting, drifting, prey to the eddies and currents. Often I kept my eyes closed and it seemed that I had always been drifting along like this; the rest of my life had been but a dream.

I turned my head to the left – next to Paiju Peak I seemed to see the elegant ridge of the Geislerspitzen, and a little further away, the Ruefen, at the foot of which lies our house. And Uschi, she was there too, but distant. I could not reach her, but I saw her clearly.

Another moment and these pictures too slip by, hidden by the passing banks as the river moves on. I look up again. Left and right in the dull light of day, the landscape glides past – mountains, mountains without redemption.

DIARY OF THE EXPEDITIONS

Taken from daily diary excerpts and newspaper reports

LHOTSE SOUTH FACE

1972	Reinhold Messner requests permission from the Nepal Government for an ascent of Lhotse.
1973	Alessandro Gogna receives permission from the Nepal Government for an ascent of Lhotse from the south. He hands this permission over to the Italian Alpine Club (CAI).
1973	Decision of the CAI to launch a national-Italian expedition for a difficult eight thousander face. The CAI assigns the task of reconnaissance and planning to Riccardo Cassin.
1974 Pre-monsoon	Riccardo Cassin and Roberto Sorgato reconnoitre the South Face of Lhotse (8511 m). While ascending to the upper Lhotse Glacier, Cassin discovers a possible and justifiable route in the fall line of the 3500 m South Face.
1974 Summer	Reinhold Messner just returned from an unsuccessful attempt of the South Face of Makalu, requests, via the Pakistan Embassy in Rome, permission to make a two-man expedition to Hidden Peak (Gasherbrum I) (8068 m), with Broad Peak and Gasherbrum II as alternatives.
1974 Post-monsoon	Riccardo Cassin undertakes a second reconnaissance to the South Face of Lhotse. On a flight round the summit he sees a possible way to carry out his idea: a direttissima up the South Face of Lhotse.
1974 Late Autumn	Riccardo Cassin and the Committee of the CAI choose the participants of the Lhotse South Face Expedition. Reinhold Messner is invited. He accepts with two conditions: 1. No Expedition Agreement and 2. Final choice of route to be made at Base Camp.
1974/5 Winter	First meeting of the team. Planning and procuring of the equipment. Main work undertaken by Cassin.
January	Discussion about the route with journalists in Milan. Reinhold Messner is totally against the summit fall line route, although he has only seen pictures of the face. He proposes a less direct route on the left side of the wall, via a huge ice ramp leading to the arete between Nuptse and Lhotse, then crossing to the north side and following the Swiss route to the summit.
February	Preparations for the Lhotse Expedition in Milan and Lecco.
11 March	Flight of the Lhotse Expedition from Milan in two Hercules aircraft from the Italian Army.
12 March	Arrival in Katmandu.
13-19 March	Sorting out bureaucratic requirements in Nepalese capital. The first participants fly to Lukla.
20 March	All team members in Namche Bazar. The Sherpas are equipped.
21 March - 3 April	March-in to Base Camp (about 5300 m) at foot of Lhotse South Face, with 600 loads. Much rain and snow. Several days of enforced delay.

4 April	Franco Chierego, expedition doctor, becomes severely ill and has to be carried back to Dingboche. Ignazio Piussi accompanies him via helicopter to Katmandu, where he is taken to hospital.
5 April	The party decides on the ramp route.
5-7 April	First reconnaissance and placing of fixed ropes on the face.
8 April	Reinhold Messner and party establish Camp I at about 6000 m.
9-11 April	More rope fixing above Camp I.
12 April	Aldo Anghileri decides to leave the expedition and return to Italy. Reinhold Messner and Aldo Leviti set up Camp II at about 6600 m.
10-16 April	Ignazio Piussi, Det and Gigi Alippi, Arcari and other members of the party construct a rope railway to carry loads of up to 15 kg, (suspension and hauling ropes) between Camp I and a projecting rock at about 6400 m. This obviated the carrying of heavy loads by the Sherpas over difficult terrain.
18 April	Sereno Barbacetto and Allessandro Gogna climb up to 6900 m, attaching fixed ropes at the steepest parts.
19 April	Snowing on the face. An avalanche falls close to Base Camp about midnight.
20 April	A large ice avalanche starts from the middle of the face (about 6500 m) and completely destroys Base Camp. Four Sherpas injured. Radio call for all members to leave the face and return to Base Camp.
21 April	Base Camp re-sited lower down. A majority vote of all members decides to continue the assault.
22-23 April	Searching for buried expedition equipment.
24 April to 2 May	Snowing all the time. Despite this, rope railway re-started and both high camps dug out.
3 May	Det Alippi supports Reinhold Messner and Mario Curnis in forcing route to Camp III (about 7200 m) Messner and Curnis establish this camp and remain there.
4-5 May	Reinhold Messner and Mario Curnis ascend to 7500 m in order to reconnoitre a way to the summit ridge. The direct ascent is found to be too dangerous and shattered. Messner sees a better route more to the left.
6-7 May	Alessandro Gogna and Sereno Barbacetto try the left-hand route up the summit wall and finally attain a height of 7500 m.
7-8 May	Aldo Leviti replaces Gogna at Camp III and remains there. During the night the tent is crushed by an avalanche. Emergency bivouac of Barbacetto and Leviti at camp site.
8-13 May	Snowing every day. All attempts to dig out high camps fail.
13 May	Decision to abandon expedition.
13-20 May	Reinhold Messner descends to the valley to meet his wife who intends to come up to Base Camp with her sister and a friend. Start of dismantling high Camps. Reinhold Messner arrives at Base Camp with his wife and the two girls and ascends once again to Camp II with Alessandro Gogna to collect tents, sleeping bags and oxygen cylinders.
20 May	Expedition leaves Base Camp.
21-25 May	Descent to Lukla via Solo Khumbu. Long delay in Katmandu.
11 June	Arrival at Milan.

HIDDEN PEAK NORTH WEST FACE

1975

20 June	Final decision by Reinhold Messner to undertake a two-man expedition to Hidden Peak.
21-30 June	Preparatory work for this mini expedition.
1 July	Reinhold Messner leaves Villnöss. Travels to Mayrhofen in the Zillertal. Farewell party.
2-3 July	Reinhold Messner and Peter Habeler travel to Munich. Flight via Frankfurt to Karachi and on to Rawalpindi, the capital of Pakistan.
4-11 July	Rawalpindi. Bureaucratic delays.
12 July	Flight to Skardu. Twelve porters hired.
13-24 July	March to Base Camp (5100 m) on the Abruzzi Glacier.
27 July	First reconnaissance into the Gasherbrum Valley.
28-30 July	Descent to Base Camp. Bad weather.
31 July to 2 August	Second reconnaissance. Ascent to the Gasherbrum La. (about 6600 m).
3-7 August	Resting in Base Camp. Bad weather.
8 August	Ascent to first bivouac in the Gasherbrum Valley. (5900 m).
9 August	Reinhold Messner and Peter Habeler climb lower part of North West Face of Hidden Peak. Second bivouac (7100 m)
10 August	Ascent to summit of Hidden Peak (8068 m) and descent to second bivouac.
11 August	Descent to bivouac site in Gasherbrum Valley.
12 August	Descent to Base Camp.
13-20 August	Return march from Base Camp to Skardu.
21-24 August	Waiting for a flight to Rawalpindi.
25 August	Flight to Rawalpindi.
26 August	To Ministry of Tourism to report expedition achievements.
27 August	Return flight to Europe.